Published by Daniel Starża Smith via CreateSpace (www.createspace.com)

Printed in the United States of America

ISBN-13: 978-1495228520
ISBN-10: 1495228525

"Where The Devil Says Goodnight"

Exile To Siberia, 1940–1946

Alfreda Starża-Miniszewska

Translated by Daniel Starża Smith

CONTENTS

AUTHOR'S FOREWORD

This book chronicles the history of my family during the Second World War. We were ethnic Poles living in Belarus when war broke out. One day, Soviet soldiers burst into our houses, tearing us away from our homes and exiling us into the frozen depths of Siberia, to work or to die. Many of my family members lost their lives – to hunger, to extreme cold or to physical oppression – but we never gave up. I have written this book to preserve the memories of those who died and record the heroism of those who refused to give in to the Soviet regime. The war brought with it many horrors, and we must ensure that the stories of those who suffered are preserved. My narrative is based on personal memories, library research and notes from extensive discussions with family members. I was also able to draw on the memories of my sister Zosia, who left written records of her experience; I signal in the chapter titles or headings when she takes over the story.

DERBYSHIRE, 2014

INTRODUCTION – FAMILY BACKGROUND

My family originates from the Lublin area of Poland. My father, Wacław Łukasik, came from Sieńciaszka, two kilometres from Łuków, and my mother, Józefa Stasiak, from the village of Góry, in the district of Markuszów. My father's father, Stanisław Łukasik, was a carpenter and builder who also owned a farm. His wife, Anna, who came from Smyk, died giving birth to my father, their only child, on 21 May 1893. Stanisław then married Anna's sister, Maria – so Maria was both aunt and stepmother to Wacław, and brought him up from birth. Stanisław and Maria had four children of their own, two sons, Jan and Antoni, and two daughters, Maria and Leokadia. My father loved his sisters but did not get on well with his brothers, and he hated his step-mother. He couldn't wait to leave the house as soon as he could.

**My mother and father with Zdzichu and Zosia in 1928.
My mother is pregnant with me.**

My father took well to learning and, Maria told me, he taught all the children in the village to read and write in his house. After completing his studies he starting working in a pharmacy in Łuków. Here he served clients, preparing some of the prescriptions himself, and dreamed of becoming a pharmacist in his own right. Unfortunately the First World War ruined his plans. He was 21 when it broke out, and was conscripted to the Czar's army, although he didn't serve for a long time. My father shot off two of the fingers on his right hand so that he didn't have to fight against other Poles, and was consequently discharged from the army as an invalid. Maria told me all this, too. These days we might call him a conscientious objector.

After his release from the army my father joined the police. One of his duties was to search for deserters from the army, but sometimes he protected conscripts who had fled. One of these was one of my mother's brothers, although I don't know which. While pretending to conduct a search for him, he met my mother, then a beautiful 18 year old, and fell in love. They married in 1920, when my mum was only 19. My Ciocia Helena told me that he made a very handsome policeman, and looked fantastically smart in his navy blue uniform and white gloves. She told me she was jealous that her sister had such a good-looking fiancé! By the time they had had two children, Zosia and Zdzichu, my mother was putting pressure on him to leave the police, saying it was dogs' work, and very dangerous. He listened to her, and took an office job in the Union for Invalids in Łuków.

In 1926, my mother's father, Leonard Stasiak, settled in the eastern borderlands of Kresy Wschodnie (also called *Polesie*, "beyond the forest"), and in 1927 my parents joined them. They all lived together with my grandparents, and the Stasiaks' youngest son, Ignac.

I was born there, as was my younger brother, Tadzio. My mother named me after her favourite teacher, whom she thought a particularly beautiful and helpful woman.

My mother's teacher Alfreda, my namesake.

I remember very little of my father, as he died when I was only four years old, and Tadzio was only two. However, I remember very clearly how he lay in his coffin on a bench in front of the house. Somebody lifted me up and said "Children, say goodbye to daddy," and told me to kiss him. Afterwards, I remember the knocking as they nailed the coffin lid shut. Later on, when I was about seven, I would go by myself to the church in Wierzchowice, and to the cemetary, and looked for my father's grave, and couldn't find it. I was very sad, and cried, partly because I could see that those children with fathers were much happier than I was, and had better lives. Other children always talked about their fathers – as soon as something didn't suit them they would say, "I'll tell my dad!" We always had to submit to the other children because we didn't have a father to run to.

4

My father Wacław in 1915, aged around 21. I damaged
the picture as a child, in anger at him dying and leaving us.

My father's older sister, Marysia, with her husband and daughters,
Władzia, Maria and Halina. They lived in Zielona Góra in Poland,
and were not part of the deportation.

**My father's younger sister, Lodzia. On either side
of her are their brothers Antek (left) and Janek (right).**

Once, on a Sunday, after mass, my mother took Tadzio and me
to the cemetary and showed us my father's grave. It was surrounded by
a wooden fence, and had a large wooden cross. I felt peace and calm
knowing where my father rested. A tall leafy tree, perhaps a birch,
shimmered above the grave.

She told us to kneel, and together we recited "*wieczny
odpoczynek*" (a Polish prayer of peace), and we asked my father to
protect us. She told us that he was in Heaven with the angels, right by
the side of God, and that God would listen to him if he asked for our
care. I believed it. From that time, whenever I went to the graveyard, I
always cried and worried that he had left us behind, and chosen Heaven
over us, even though we needed him, and all my cousins had fathers. I
remember all this very clearly, and now as an older person understand
very well the suffering of that half-orphaned little girl, how sad and
painful it must have been for her without her father.

All her cousins – Krysia, Wanda, Balbina, Urszula and Kamila – had fathers, and she didn't. They were all rich, because their fathers were in charge of this area, strong powerful men, and resourceful with it. They had servants, men and women, and employed cattle herdsmen, whom they could order around. But that little girl had only her mother, who had to fight for the existence of her family, until at last her own father helped her to buy a house. My grandfather gave my mother some land and, a few years later, before the war, he and his wife Marianna, moved into her house, mainly because he couldn't stand living with his son Ignac any longer.

My mother Józefa came from a large, rich family of landowners from Góry in the Lublin area. My grandfather, Leonard Stasiak, married Marianna from the Piech family, and they had 10 children – six sons and four daughters. The oldest son, Franciszek, became mayor of Kałuszyn, which is not far from Warsaw.

**Franciszek Stasiak, Mayor of Kałuszyn,
seated centre in the light-coloured coat.**

Another son, Stanisław, was a politician and patriot who fought against the Czar's regime, and was later punished for this "crime" with exile to Siberia, where he spent five years. When he returned he married Róża, and they had one son, Ludomir. After the war, Stanisław was chosen as an MP for the Lublin region; a close friend of President Bolesław Bierut, he worked for liberated Poland into his old age. Ludomir Stasiak was an economist and a political activist particularly dedicated to peasants' rights. He held many key positions in the Polish government including MP for Sejm (1952-85) and served as Secretary of State (*sekretarz Rady Panstwa PRL*) from 1969 to 1980. He received a state burial with military honours at Cmentarz Wojskowy na Powązkach, the famous Polish military cemetary in Warsaw.

On the left is Ludomir Stasiak, standing next to his wife Łucja, who took the name Alina when she was a Partisan fighter, and their daughter Barbara. On the right is Stanisław, standing next to his wife Róża.

The third son, Bolesław, fought against the Germans, and was tortured and murdered in the Majdanek concentration camp in Lublin. He lived in Nałęczów with his wife Janina and three children, Alfreda, Teodozja and Kazimierz. My grandparents' fourth son, Jan, became a rich landowner. He finished agricultural college and owned a fruit nursery, where young students from the college would learn their trade. Jan lived with his family in Suszki, in the administrative district of Wierzchowice in the region of Brześć nad Bugiem. On 10 February 1940, he was deported by the Soviets to Siberia with his whole family – his wife Anna and their three daughters Krysia, Wanda and Balbina. After six years of exile he returned to Poland, settling in Sitno, in the Bydgoszcz region, where he lived until he died.

The fifth son, Władysław Stasiak, was a landowner and lived with his wife Aniela and his three sons and one daughter (Włodek, Genek, Witek and Róża) in a village called Dys near Lublin.

The sixth son, Ignac, was the youngest of these offspring. He lived with his parents in Suszki. He married Julia, and they had three children, Ludek, Basia and Alinka. In February 1940, together with the family, he was exiled to Siberia. On this bitter journey his youngest daughter Alinka died, as I describe below, and later on his wife Julia and his newborn son died in childbirth. In June 1943, the First Division of the Polish Army was formed, named after Tadeusz Kościuszko (1746-1817), a Polish war hero. Ignac joined the Kościuszko division, and was killed in the Battle of Warsaw in 1945. His children Ludek and Basia were taken to an orphanage then brought to Poland after the war.

My grandparents' oldest daughter was called Felicia. She married Franciszek Pawelec, and they lived in their family village, Góry, near Puławy, Lublin. They had a daughter, Zosia and a son, Stasiu.

Hipolit Król, and my uncles, Janek and Stanisław.

Karolina was the next oldest daughter. She married Hipolit Król, a war veteran, and they settled in Suszki. They had four children, Adolek, Bolesław, Jan and Stasia. In 1940, with the rest of the family, they were exiled to Siberia, where Hipolit died of starvation. Two of their sons, Bolesław and Jan, joined the Kościuszko army, and fortunately lived through battles with the German occupiers. At the end of the war, they moved to the countryside in Poland together with their families. Bolesław Król was promoted to the rank of Captain, and remained in the army at the end of the war, settling not far from Włocławek, but Jan Król settled in Gorzów. They both married and had children. Adolek died from appendicitis aged 21, during his military service. Stasia married Konstantin Walesiak, and they settled in Międzylesie, near the Czech border, in the county of Walbrzych. They adopted a daughter, Elzunia. The life of Bolesław Król ended in particularly unpleasant circumstances, described in Chapter 10.

The youngest of my grandparents' daughters, Helena, married another veteran from the war against the Bolsheviks, Marceli Kitajewski, who had been awarded land for his service and bravery, and they settled in Zwody, in Brest-Litovsk. They had two sons, Ryszard and Ludomir, and two daughters, Urszula and Kamila. On 10 February 1940, they were all deported to Siberia, where they stayed until the formation of General Anders' army, which Helena's husband joined, taking his family with him. In 1942, they left the Soviet Union. They travelled through Persia, Lebanon and Egypt, before reaching England and settling in London. Helena died in London aged 100 in 2005, five months after receiving a telegram from Queen Elizabeth II.

Kresy Wschodnie-Polesie: our family's estates before exile

Kresy Wschodnie-Polesie was an area beyond the River Bug. In Polish, "beyond the Bug" is "Za Bugiem", which is what we called the area. During Poland's war against the Bolsheviks in 1919-20, General Józef Pilsudski regained this territory for the Poles. Nearby villages, large and long-established, where the houses were covered with thatched rooves, were predominently Belarusian and Ukrainian, a fact indicative of the tussles over land that had gone on for many years. The terrain beyond the Bug comprised mainly of wet marshlands and great forests, but there were also arable fields and pastures. In order to reclaim more arable land people chopped down the forests and built canals to drain the wetlands.

The Polish government, wanting to settle as many Poles there as possible, granted plots of land for free to former soldiers who had fought against the Bolsheviks. They kept land prices low to tempt other Poles to move there, and many duly migrated. My grandfather,

Leonard, found himself among them, with the majority of his family. In 1926, he sold his estate in Lublin, and bought a great expanse of land in Suszki, in the Wysoko Litewskie district. He divided this land between his five sons, and married his two daughters to former military men, as explained above.

My parents, with their eldest two children, also joined them, and I and my brother were born there in 1928 and 1930 respectively. This Stasiak family settlement was very well-situated by the main road, which led

The Stasiak family in Suszki. Ciocia Karolina is in the back row in the white shirt, next to her husband Hipolit Król. Bolek is in the middle row holding the baby, Ludek; to the right of him sit his sister Stasia, my Ciocia Hela, my mother Józia, her sister-in-law Andzia, holding her youngest daughter Balbina. On Bolek's other side is Julia, Wujek Ignac's wife; the baby on her lap is Alinka, and the other child is Basia. Wujek Janek is lying on the ground; behind his legs sits his daughter Krysia, and Wanda is in front of his shoulder. I'm next to Wanda, with my hands touching the ground; next to me is my cousin Ryszard, and behind me his sister Kamila, Hela's children.

to the nearby town of Wierzchowice. A beautiful Russian Orthodox church stood in this town, and a Catholic church, which we attended, had recently been built. I was Christened and later took my First Communion there. There was also a town hall in Wierzchowice, and several shops and taverns run by Jews.

On the other side of our Suszki land lay two large, old Belarusian villages – Brzozówka and Jesionówka. Boys from these villages would fall upon our lads all the time, and beat them up. A friend of my older brother was so badly injured in one eye by a knife during one of these attacks that he lost his sight. When the Russians took over our territory, these Belarusian and Ukrainian settlements built triumphal arches for them, and welcomed the Soviet Army as their saviours from Polish "*pany*", rich landowners.

However, there were several Belarusian families in Suszki who accepted us. Across the road lived a farmer called Trofimuk, a good man, and opposite my grandfather's house lived Wróbel, who was even nicer. I used to go to school with Wróbel's daughter Nina, and his son Ivan was a good friend of my brother Zdzichu. They were really good neighbours, and even sent us a food parcel when we were in Siberia. I remember another three Belarusian farmers who bought the farms of my three uncles, Bolesław, Stanisław and Władysław, when their wives begged to leave Suszki. Those women badly missed their home country in Lublin, and the families they had left behind. They begged their husbands to sell the farms and return to Lublin. It turned out very well that they returned when they did, otherwise even more of us would have been deported to Siberia.

The other members of the Stasiak family, however – Janek, Ignac, Karolina, Helena, our mother and my grandparents – decided to stay Za Bugiem. All of them built houses, planted vegetables and orchards, cultivated fields and were contented with what they had. Our mother, in the years following the death of her husband, also built a house, and we moved there from our grandparents' home.

My sister Zosia graduated from agricultural college and returned back home. She planted a great many flowers and vegetable gardens around our house, taking great care of them all herself. Multicoloured *malvas* surrounded our house, and strongly scented flowering peas wrapped themselves all over our fences. *Goździki* (carnations) and *maciejka* (night-scented stocks) filled the air with their aromas. As night fell, wonderful smells would fill the house through the open windows. In front of the house stood a big wooden bench, where we would gather as a family in the warm, quiet evenings, with only the sound of croaking frogs carrying in from the surrounding fields. It was so enchanting that you could hardly bring yourself to go back inside. Indeed, Tadek and I would often fall asleep out there on the bench... until my mother shouted that a bogeyman would come and get us. Of course, hearing this we would then jump up and run into the house, absolutely terrified!

The nearest we got to an actual bogeyman in those days was one old man who asked my mother for permission to cook his dinner in our kitchen. I'll never forget how he cooked *kasza* (barley) on pieces of meat. He poured it into a big bowl, and it looked incredibly appetising and smelled so nice. He ate it smacking his lips, making us even more hungry to watch him – but he didn't invite us to join him, and devoured it all by himself! After he had gone, we asked our mother to make us "old man *kasza*" just like that.

We owned two cows, horses, pigs, geese, chickens, a dog and some cats. Local boys would come to visit Zosia, asking our mother if she could come out dancing with them. Her friends would come on their bicycles, many recent fellow graduates of the agricultural college. They were beautifully dressed, and I greatly admired their navy blue velvet hats, embroidered with ears of corn in gold. I envied my sister her lovely friends. In the evening the youngsters would walk or cycle along the main road, while the frogs sang in the nearby marshes and meadows. In summer, the evenings were warm, light and very pleasant.

Winter was very different. Evenings were long and dark – although never boring. People would gather to slice cabbages and put them into barrels for salting and fermentation, so that we would have plenty to eat over winter. Or they would pluck geese and chickens, preparing the feathers for the stuffing of pillows. While they worked they would either sing, or tell stories, perhaps ghost stories, mysteries or scary folk tales.

My Babcia Marianna knew many stories like this, and the way she told them sent goosebumps of terror running up our arms. Everything she said struck us children as absolutely true. The scariest stories were about people who had got lost in the marshes, moaning in the mists and begging for help. Others were about devils who tricked travellers and led them into the marshes, where they drowned and were never seen again. Other devils would stop horse and carts and ask for lifts, then paralyse the horse and drive them mad until they tore away from their shackles and reins, fleeing and abandoning their masters in the middle of nowhere, far from home. Sometimes I thought I'd die from fright!

I was seven, and used to return home from my friend Zuzia Kopeć in the evening, along a cobbled path between the meadows. I knew it well because half the meadows belonged to us, and our horses grazed there. But there were also marshes all around, where waterlilies and yellow flowers, *kaczeńce* (marigolds), grew. We would often be led towards the marshes by these beautiful flowers, and would jump from reed-bed to reed-bed looking for duck eggs. Wujek Ignac would sometimes forget to bring his horses back from that pasture and they would stay overnight, and it was always fine. But one time everything was different – I had overstayed, and night had fallen much faster than I had expected.

Zuzia had a brother who was a bit older, and his friends used to come and visit him. Another friend, Czesia Kielakówna and Zosia Niedziółkówna both used to come too, so there was quite a gathering of young people, and we were all able to play together. We had been playing a game of "hosts", pretending to make tea and cakes for guests. Zuzia's mother aways prepared something delicious for us, like bread with honey, or sour cream and sugar, or biscuits or fruit, depending on the season. After our game, we would run around and play hide and seek. When children are playing nicely together, of course, they forget all about the time. Suddenly I noticed that it was getting dark; I dropped my toys and ran quickly home.

A cobbled road ran nearby, and I sprinted down it as the night got darker and darker. A mist started to rise from the meadows, and suddenly I heard from the depths of the meadow, a metal trotting – someone, or something, weighed down with chains, seemed to be chasing me. I was terrified and ran quicker and quicker, convinced that it was one of the devils from Babcia's stories. I managed to reach our garden, completely out of breath, but the chains were just behind me, almost touching me. I realised it was the clopping of hooves and the whinnying of a horse – it was our horse, Gniady, who had recognised me and had run over to me in pleasure to say hello. In fact, he overtook me and got to our fence first. The poor horse, forgotten by his owner, had pulled out his stake from the ground and ran home. This realisation didn't mean I was any less terrified, and I have been scared of horses ever since, even to this day.

My Babcia Marianna was a very clever woman. She knew how to host, could talk politics, and was something of a medicine woman, treating humans and animals, delivering children, and carrying out minor surgery on new-borns if they had small defects. She had boxes with rudimentary surgical tools and nowadays she would probably be called a midwife. My mother told me how Marianna removed a sixth toe from one new-born child, and would cut the connective tissue under

My grandparents, Marianna and Leonard.

the tongue of children with speech defects, in order to help "loosen their tongue". People were always coming to fetch her, or bringing crying children to her to massage or stretch. She carried out all sorts of funny procedures that might now be called "alternative medicine" – burning sheep's wool and mumbling "spells".

Young children in the countryside occasionally had abscesses on their body, and she would apply leeches to them, which she kept in a jar. An alternative was "*bańki*", small glass baubles that were heated up then applied to the skin. She made herbal medicines too, for insomnia, headaches etc. You had to travel a long way to get to the doctor, and it was very expensive, so people came to "Babka Marianna", who helped them for free. Those who could would give a donation, those who could not did not have to, and she didn't ask.

The countryside was beautiful, but always reminded me of the day in May when my father died. He loved lilac, so Zosia, Urszula and I went to pick some for him. As we walked back a large bee buzzed insistently around the lilac blossoms in my arms. Just then, a boy called Staszek Maj ran up crying "Hurry, hurry, your dad is dying." By the time we returned, he had died. Could that bee have been my father's soul as it departed his body, coming to say one last goodbye to his daughters?

When I was about nine years old, we moved from our grandparents' house to our own home, and a year before the war, our grandparents moved in with us. My grandfather died of a heart-attack shortly after our exile to Siberia. My grandmother lived alone and lonely for five more years. The people who she used to help now looked after her until her death, shortly before the end of the war.

CHAPTER 1 – SEPTEMBER 1939

September 1939 – the Second World War erupted, truly plunging Poland into Hell. First, the Germans arrived: the skies rumbled with the noise of Nazi planes, their wings flashing the black tattoo of the Swastika. Explosions seemed to surround us, as the invading airforce dropped bombs on train stations and other targets in the area. They sent units of German soldiers to our road; Germans stopped at each of our houses, to grab something to eat or wash themselves in our wells. They chatted away in German, and if people didn't understand them the soldiers would draw what they meant in the sand. They smiled and laughed with us children and offered us chocolate, so they didn't seem so bad. Besides, they never stayed in the same place for long; as they moved on along the main road their traces disappeared behind them.

Not long after this, however, the scene was soon to change. Instead of "black ravens" came "grey starlings" – the Russian army. They were greeted with enthusiasm by the ethnic Russians in our Belarusian villages, as if they were some kind of liberators, freeing them from their "Polish masters". (There were long-standing tensions in the region dating back to the 1385 unification of Poland, Lithuania, Belarus and Ukraine.)

So once again an army passed through our world, not causing anyone any harm… and then it fell quiet again. The elders said that Stalin and Hitler had divided Poland in two between them, and that on the Russian side – our side – a new Communist order would be established. In the beginning nothing changed noticeably, except that the Russian language was introduced at school. Our White Russian neighbours did no harm to us, as they had in other regions – for example, those where the Ukrainian villages were situated, so nobody suspected anything tragic. In this rather gentle manner autumn passed and winter approached.

February 1940 – it was incredibly cold and snowdrifts mounted halfway up the houses. We had to dig tunnels to the barn and main road, because otherwise there was no passage. Hardly anybody looked in on our small village, and we knew little about what was going on in the rest of the world. We carried on with our normal lives.

In the evenings my mother prepared dough for bread the next day, and washed linen was soaked in the *balia*, then soaked in cold water overnight, after which it would be rinsed and hung outside in the fresh air to dry. Our only dog, Burek, began acting strangely: he didn't want to eat, would nuzzle himself against your legs, and would howl mournfully at night, until the cows lowed in sympathy. We sensed an atmosphere which unsettled us in our hearts. Could the animals have sensed something?

Deportation

On 10 February 1940, came the first and most extensive deportation of Poles into the depths of Russia, organised by the Russian secret police, the NKVD. On this day, over a hundred thousand families were taken away from Kresy Wschondnie, and all their property was confiscated. The deportation was secret, and extremely organised. The Russians transported the Poles to various dismal holes throughout Russia – under the Arctic Circle (where I would end up), on and beyond the Urals, all along Siberia, as far as the Far East: Vladivostok, Sahalin, and the Kazakhstan Steppes. The intention was clearly to exile these people for good. They sent innocent people away to their extermination, depriving them not only of their country and their property, but also their very humanity. They settled us in the deep Taiga in the Archangel region and near Archangel itself, the main port on the White Sea.

On 10 February the agents of our deportation arrived at six o'clock in the morning, when it was still dark; Burek's barking awoke us, and after a short while there was heavy knocking at the door. We jumped to our feet, terribly frightened, but no-one dared approach the door. My older brother Zdzichu (aged 16) was at Wujek Janek's, and in the house was mum, my 19-year-old sister Zosia, nine-year-old brother Tadzio, and myself, not quite 12. My grandparents, both well advanced in age, were also there. Naturally, we were very scared. Our first thought was that some sort of bandits had come to ransack the house – but then, bandits fell on the rich, or those they had had dealings with. But in our house there lived only a widow, with four children and elderly parents. Clearly there was nothing here to steal. The banging at the door was getting ever stronger and more insistent, and it seemed they would soon break down the door. Suddenly we heard a familiar voice – that of our neighbour, Mr Wróbel. My mother went to the door and asked what was going on. She heard him talking to someone in Russian, then he shouted: "Open the door." Mum did as he said, and a handful of Russian soldiers barged in, with rifles strapped across their shoulders. One of them wore a white fur coat, a fur hat emblazoned with the Russian star, and was carrying a pistol: he was from the NKVD. Standing among them was our neighbour and closest friend, Mr Wróbel, who was commanded to take us to the station.

First the NKVD-man shouted: "Hands up!" (*ruki vverkh*), while the other soldiers searched us for weapons. Next, the officer read out an order of Stalin's, known as an *ukaz*, which dealt with our special "resettlement", and declared that in two hours we should be ready to hit the road. Mum asked where they were taking us to. He replied: *"Poka na stantsiiu a potom nie znaiu"* – to the station for now, and after that I don't know. Mum began to cry, and ran around the room not knowing what to do.

My grandparents had stayed in bed throughout all this commotion; they were old, over 80, and frail. The officer ordered them to be woken and dressed; my grandmother was ready to acquiesce to the orders, but grandfather said he would never move out of this place, indeed that if the soldiers wanted, they should shoot them on the spot, because they weren't going anywhere. To be fair to them, the soldiers didn't carry out an execution, but left my grandparents in peace. After all, they had nothing to gain from killing them. The NKVD-man returned to my mother and said: *"Sobiraities skorei, sobiraities"* – get ready quickly – and told mum to take the washing from the water, rinse it, and put it in a sack. We would need it, he explained, it would come in useful. He told mum to take flour, barley and bacon and even allowed her to kill a few chickens, so that there would be something to eat on the journey. A skilled dressmaker, she also packed her sewing machine on the sledge. You could see he pitied us: my mother was young, 39 years old, a widow, still looking after small children, and on top of that had elderly parents under her care. Perhaps he thought, why, for what reason, are they deporting these people? What have they done?

Meanwhile, my brother Zdzichu, who had stayed at Wujek Janek's overnight, ran home breathlessly, saying that they were also deporting Wujek Janek and Wujek Ignac, and that everyone was already travelling in our direction to form a single convoy to the station.

Wujek Janek didn't know they were deporting our side of the family too, and begged the commandant deporting him to let him say goodbye to his parents and leave them a jar of honey (Wujek Janek had a large apiary which produced a lot of honey). I find it very strange that they allowed my Wujek to do this – even though he had just been held at gunpoint while he was packing. When Wujek Janek gave his dad the honey, the officer in charge of us took the jar and gave it to me, saying: "*Beri, devchonka, med tebe prigoditsia, a starikam ne nuzhno, oni naelis' ego mnogo w svoei zhizni*" – take it little girl, honey will be useful for you; these old people don't need it, they have had lots of it in their lives. Until today, I find it hard to believe that this NKVD-man showed so much heart for a little girl whom he was sending to her extermination. Maybe somewhere in Russia he had his own little children, and maybe he was missing them?

While the soldiers loaded our belongings onto the sledges, Tadzio and I went to the barn to say goodbye to our animals. The dog Burek, and the cows, Pisana and Mećka, behaved very anxiously, as if they knew that they were seeing us for the last time. Burek hugged himself to us, wagging his tail, whining as if he was crying. It was very sad for us to leave our intelligent animals – our faithful dog, and our cows, who had fed us with their own milk, and which we in turn had fed in the flowery meadows. Now, at our separation, they licked us with their rough tongues, and gazed upon us with almost tearful eyes. At least Babcia and Dziadek stayed, so there was someone to look after them for some time.[1]

---

[1] Pisana was a beautiful cow, with white and red patches. She was very strong, and when the weather was hot, she would lift up her tail and run away from the pasture, and through the marshy meadows ran away from us to the cow herd from the Belarusian village Brzozówka. After our departure, when

After we were taken away, they were cared for by a wonderful man called Jan Sulima. He was a neighbour, a true gentleman who had a family coat of arms. I think he loved my mother. He actually pleaded to come with us to Siberia but was not permitted. Jan Sulima would later bury both my grandparents and save some family heirlooms for our return – portraits of my grandparents and two beautiful wooden trunks.

The journey to the station

After loading the baggage and ourselves onto the sledge, we began to move. It was extremely cold and the snow was falling heavily. It was hard for the horses to trudge through the snowdrifts and pull a laden sledge at the same time: even they had to stop, from time to time. At the front rode the NKVD-man, then us, and after us Wujek Janek. Behind him were soldiers with rifles, keeping guard so that nobody ran away. We passed our school, never to see it again. The officer stopped and told mum that the load was too heavy for the horses, and she had to offload her sewing machine. Mum did not want to do it, because she knew her sewing could save us from starvation. However, her pleas were of no help. The soldiers took it from her and threw it into the snow, where many similar machines already lay, along with bikes, parcels and boxes. I have little doubt that all this was later packed up and sent off to Russia.

Sometime in the afternoon we were already at the railway station Wysoko-Litewskie, around 12km from our colony Suszki.

Dziadek died, and Babcia was weak and couldn't take care of the animals, someone took Pisana for himself. After the war, this man moved from Polesie to Pomorze, and took Pisana with him. And it transpired that after the war we were also settled on Pomorze. Jan Sulima told us where our Pisana was, and mum won her back through the courts, which we were very happy about. This was the only thread that linked us with our old past.

They threw us into terrible, filthy and freezing cattle wagons, locked
from the outside with iron bolts; through the night, this train carried us
to Brześć on the river Bug, where there was a main railway station, and
where our train was incorporated into one long carriage-train (which
in Russian was called an *eszelon*). This travelled onwards towards its
destination: Russia.

In the wagon

I don't know if all the wagons were the same, but I do know what
ours was like. It was a normal cattle wagon, with sliding doors on both
sides, but only one opening – the other ones were shut "*na amen*" (for
good). In order to adapt them for the carrying of people, our captors had
made several "improvements". In the middle of the wagon was a fixed
iron stove, with a chimney going through the roof so the smoke could
escape. The sides of the wagons were divided into two parts, the bottom
for luggage, and the top for people. To one side was a hole, which was
used as a toilet.

Our wagon was very cold, crowded and dark. On our side there
were about twenty people; there were the five of us, five of my uncle's
family, and another family called Niedźwiedź, with many children.
These people had two dwarf children. We had never seen dwarves
before. My mother called one of these boys across to our group and
wrapped him in a feather quilt, because he was sitting by himself,
curled up and shivering from the extreme cold. The truth emerged only
later, when mum asked him, "How old are you, little boy?" When he
replied that he was eighteen, everyone in the carriage burst out laughing
– and mum felt very embarrassed! This small incident relieved the

oppressive atmosphere a little. One of the men made a fire in the stove and the mothers could fed their children and put them to sleep.

The train paused in Brest station so they could refit our train to the Russian tracks, so we sat there for quite a while. Complete darkness fell. We had no light other than what little emanated from the stove. The children cried, and wanted to go to the toilet but were afraid to approach the hole in the floor in case they fell through. Despite the burning iron stove the carriage was still bitterly cold: the walls were covered with frost, and more grey frost covered the small long window along the top of one of the walls. Fortunately, there was wood and some coal, and someone was always keeping watch to ensure the fire didn't go out. Those in charge came to check the list of prisoners. They reclosed the carriages from outside, and with a great knocking and screeching the train moved on into the unknown.

Journey into the unknown

The *eszelon* crawled along slowly, with a huge screeching and juddering. The unfortunate prisoners within groaned in accompaniment, with the crying of children, prayer or sorrowful singing of religious songs. In this manner, we proceeded at a torturously slow pace. The train would move for a while, or stop and sit for a long time, but the door never opened, and no-one gave us bread or water so we made water ourselves with snow: my sister dropped a pail through the window on a string, collected some of the plentiful snow alongside the tracks, which we then melted and boiled, cooked food and washed ourselves. The chickens which we had been allowed to kill and take with us came in very useful now. We cooked barley soup (*krupnik*) with these chickens and everyone had some of it. The jar of honey which the

NKVD-man gave to me instead of to my grandparents also served as nourishment for everybody, especially the children.

The toilet situation was much worse. Children went when they had to (their parents held them to prevent them falling through the hole), while the older people tended to wait for night-time. But when someone really needed to go, then he or she would crouch over the hole, and the smell of excrement spread through the wagon. Meanwhile the train knocked, juddered and whistled, but didn't stop. Only on the third day, having already arrived on Soviet soil, it halted at a bigger station for a little longer than usual. The metal whined as the guards finally opened the door. In front of the *eszelon*, soldiers walked with their rifles slung across their shoulders. For the first time they gave us *kipiatok* – that is, boiled water – and bread. They allowed us to leave our confinement and carry out our physical needs in the fresh air – but in the presence of guards who were laughing at us and rushing us along.

But who were we to them? The Polish exiles, Polish *kułaki*, members of the landowning class no longer protected by the old law... we were prisoners transported in cattle wagons, as if we were livestock, not people. Outside, the temperature continued to fall; in the wagons it got ever colder, and the fuel was coming to an end. Death by freezing stared us in the face. The frost was unbearable; the walls of the carriage were iced over, because people's bodies, and the heat from the stove, had turned the frost into full ice, which then melted, and the water poured onto the floor. If you didn't wipe this water up in time it too froze and formed a sheet of ice.

People felt at the end of their wits, and started to cry, shouting and calling not only for bread and water but for fuel. Our "carers" told us that we would get fuel at the next station, that prepared wood and coal were waiting for us – and they were right. At this station we were also able to get ourselves some water. There was a pump which served the steam engines, but we had to go a long way to find it.

When my sister and brother Zdzichu went for water, they saw our cousin Bolek Król by the pump. His side of the family was in another wagon. In addition, in front of the *eszelon* Zosia spotted Ciocia Hela, who stood with a small group of people in front of another carriage. From this carriage soldiers were carrying out frozen dead bodies. One old man, a neighbour of ours, had died from the cold and I realised that had my grandparents been forced to make this journey, they too would have been carried off dead. Where did they bury him? No-one will ever know.

Ciocia Hela was crying heavily, Zosia told me, because all four of her children were ill. The oldest, Urszula, was not quite 14, and the youngest, Kamila (known as Dzunia), had not yet reached seven. She also had two sons, Rysiu, about 12, and Ludek, 10. Ciocia was naturally concerned that her children were going to die like the old man. At each stop from now on, dead bodies were pulled out of the train, and unloaded either onto "sanitary machines" or simply onto lorries. And what they did with them then, God only knows.

At the next stop they ordered us to collect water, coal and firewood, and gave us some bread for the first time. I remmber that bread well – it was frozen, hard as a stone. You had to cut it in half with an axe so that it could defrost, because we were so famished we simply couldn't wait to get our ration. Now that we had been supplied with a small amount of water, fuel and bread, we moved further on, but our destination was still a mysery. Before us were huge plots of frozen land covered with a white blanket of deep snow, on which, here and there, were nests of settlements, with chimneys emitting thin wisps of smoke as a sign of life of the inhabitants of this land; or huge forests covered with thick layers of white fluffy cotton.

Very often the train stopped because the lines were so heavily obstructed with snow. When this was the case, the guards – who were dressed in warm felt boots and padded jackets – gave our men shovels and ordered them to clear the lines. On the one hand, at least they got out into the open air, but on the other hand, they didn't have warm clothes, so their feet and hands completely froze.

At one station the guards let us get out of the carriage and "invited" us to the canteen, where they gave us hot fish soup, a bit of bread and some porridge with a drop of oil, the first time they had fed us in any way properly. But I couldn't eat the soup, even though I was extremely hungry, because there were huge white fish eyes floating on the top. The Russians said "*kushai, kushai, privyknesh*" – eat, eat, you'll get used to it. But I just couldn't face it.

At this time, Ciocia Julia had a haemorrhage during her period and the Russian women saved her. They took her behind the servery on their backs, washed her and even gave her some tablets which helped her. After feeding us in this restaurant, again we were herded into the wagons, and again we travelled for some time until we got to a port on the White Sea – this was Archangel. There, white bears walked through the streets in winter, the blood froze in your veins because of the frost, and the temperature wavered between minus 35 and 40° Celsius. There they unloaded us, assembled us in a big hall and divided us between labour camps located deep in the Taiga, "where the Devil says goodnight". There was not yet a railway between the two points, and we could only get there on lorries, or tractors, or winter sledges or, in summer, on boat or raft on the river. In this latter case you had to flow with the current, because to go against the current was impossible.

Before we were unloaded onto the next path of our journey, we were given a hot meal – again, it was fish soup with floating fish eyes. This was disgusting, but people ate it because they were so hungry, and it was better to eat a plate of even this, hot, and to warm up from the inside, than to have nothing. There was also porridge with oil, and *kisiel* (jelly) with cranberries; these two were very tasty. When we were waiting for the lorries and tractors, the *severianki* (north-Russian women) distributed some more food for the next part of our journey. They had warm dumplings with cabbage, with potatoes and onion, or with mushrooms, all piled in buckets, which they gave us for free. They were crying, and made the sign of the cross over us, saying "*s Bogom*" – God be with you. Even in the heart of this Communist Russia here were good normal people, with hearts of gold. Quite often, in fact, it would happen that simple people would give us a helping hand. Without their help, not many of us would have survived.

Our family, Wujek Janek, Wujek Ignac and their families – altogether 15 people and our luggage – were loaded onto a truck. The drivers said that women and young children could sit in the truck, while men and young people had to walk. My Ciocia Julia had three little children, whom it was necessary to hold close to her so they didn't freeze. My auntie held one child, my mum held another, and the third, mum gave to Zosia. The driver looked at Zosia holding the child, and said, "*Takaia molodaia*" (such a young girl to have a baby) and helped her get onto the lorry. The lorries were not sheltered, though. Mum covered us with what she could, with a quilt or blanket, but still we were very cold. There was a strong frost, and snow was falling constantly, covering us with its white thick coat, so we looked like miserable snowmen on these lorries. My brother Zdzichu's legs froze, even in his boots, so that he actually had to remove his boots and rub his feet with the snow in order to regain feeling. The poor boy, he cried from the pain. This is how we rode for several days, as long as the lorries had a track to go on. Even here – seemingly in the middle of nowhere – Russian ladies gave us warm food, such as dumplings wrapped in towels.

The road for lorries and tractors ended, and they transferred us to sledges, which were being pulled by small but very strong horses. My sister Zosia told me all this, saying that this final stretch of the journey was the worst, on the sledges. Here are her words:

"They carried us day and night with little respite, stopping only to feed horses and give them some rest. It was frightfully cold, with a penetrating wind and a cracking frost, so that your eyes were sticking together, your face solidified, and your arms and legs became stiff as bone. We ran behind the sledges or next to them, but it was impossible. The driver cried, *"Skorei, zhdat' ne budem!"* – hurry up, we won't wait for you. Those who fell as a result of their weakness, it was the end for them. Anyone who fell over, or fell behind, was picked up and put on separate sledges, and we never saw them again. At nights they took away the people who had frozen to death – children and old people – and buried them in the snow. People were exhausted after a month's journey in carriages and on lorries. They were hungry and cold, so they dropped like flies. Oh God. Will this never end?"

We eventually stopped for rest in a shelter in the forest whose floor was strewn with straw and moss. They gave us black rye coffee and a bit of bread each, and said that it wasn't far to our new place of habitation, that tomorrow we would arrive. After this frugal meal, we threw ourselves on the hay and immediately fell asleep.

Suddenly, though, the children started to cry and throw themselves from side to side. This woke us all up, and everyone else started to scratch madly. Under our nails we felt something slimy and wet, which gave off a terrible stench – we were lying on some kind of bed-bugs! We all jumped to our feet; somebody had matches and lit a dry piece of pine tree wood – *luczywo* is a kind of pine splinter, which can be used to light a room if you don't have a lamp – Oh my God, what a horrible sight it was! Our entire bodies were smeared with blood. Running away from us and our light, were all sorts of insects, including long brown cockroaches.

It seemed like all the insects in the forest had come to attack us. Some were brown and shiny and smelly when you squashed them, others were brown-winged and with long antennae… and there were many others. Frightened by our light they escaped in several directions, crawling here and there under the covers. We started to shout and shake from fear and revulsion. I'd never seen such a disgusting sight in my life. These were a kind of bed-bug called "*tarakany*" or "*francuzy*" (little Frenchmen), which nest under the bark of trees and in moss.

Somehow, we made it through to morning, and again we mounted the sledges and continued on our way. In the evening we reached the first labour camp that would serve as our home – "Głubokij", literally "deep", deep in the Taiga.

Chapter 2 – In the Głubokij Labour Camp

What a funny name for a labour camp, Głubokij. Surely it was given that name because it was so very deeply hidden in the Taiga, "where the Devil says goodnight". A handful of old barracks stood surrounded on all sides by the mighty murmuring forest, covered with a deep layer of snow. What a strange, peopleless and threatening world was this foreign, unfamiliar, frozen land!

This labour camp was built by exiled Ukrainians in 1932, when the collectivisation of Russian satellite states was begun. They took rich landowners' possessions, and the people were banished *en masse* into the depths of Russia – and in the majority of cases they were abandoned in the forest under the naked sky. It was the banished Ukrainians who had built the barracks to which we had been brought, that is what we were told by those who had managed to survive.

I remember that camp very well, and the barrack to which we were allocated. You entered into a hall, with a window opposite, and to the side were doors to the stoves, which were situated inside the main room. By the side of these stove doors was the door to the room. When we first entered the barrack it struck me as warm, because the stoves were lit, and compared to the cold outside on our long journey, it did indeed seem very warm.

Our room (*komnata*) was designed to hold ten people – there were five of us, and five from Wujek Ignac's family. Behind one of the walls there was another *komnata*, where Wujek Janek's family was, and the family of another one of our neighbours from Suszki. On either side of the corridor was a room for twenty. On either side of the stoves were benches made of wooden planks for the whole family. These *"nary"*

were a kind of *"Madejowe loże"*, hard benches with a little straw.
My sister Zosia wrote the following about our new accommodation:

"The barrack was old, and the roof had holes in it. The
windows hardly held themselves in their frames. The doors hardly
closed. The stark wooden benches and walls were full of bed-bugs:
it was not possible to sleep because of the insects. The children cried.
Everyone in turn began to fall ill. The young medic had only aspirin to
administer for all illnesses, which soon ran out, and she couldn't help
the sick any more. The walls of the barracks were built from round
blocks, and there were halls between these blocks which we had to fill
in with moss or rags. The stoves we had to burn ourselves. Prepared
wood was not available. You had to go by yourself to get the firewood.
The snow was to waist height, and there was a terrible frost. For water
you had to go to the lake. First you had to dig through the snow and
then make a big hole in the thick ice and only then get the water. There
was there a canteen, called *"stołowaja"*, where you could get hot, black
rye coffee with sugar, porridge and a piece of bread to go with it."

On the second day, we were all called to a meeting and
everybody was allocated work. The so-called "first class workers", into
which went men and healthy women, and also young people from the
age of 16, were sent to chop down trees in the forest. Fortunately, our
mother obtained work in the kitchen, as a cook.

The death of little Alinka

As I have mentioned already, Alinka was the youngest child of Wujek
Ignac – she was only two years old. The poor girl caught a cold in this
awful long journey and became ill with pneumonia. She had a very high
temperature, and pain in her little chest and back. Her tiny lips became

hard and fiery like little coals. There was no medicine at all, apart
from aspirin and boiled water. Alinka was breathing heavily and calling
plaintively for "*mlimli*" – milk. She loved milk and in her house she
was used to drinking it straight after the cows had been milked, still
warm and fresh. Now she again cried for milk, calling, "*mlimli, mlimli*"
and holding out her hands to everyone in turn in the hope that someone,
eventually, would give her what she was begging for. From her mother,
she held out her hands to Zosia, then to me, then everyone in turn,
without end. She cried out "*mlimli, mlimli, mlimli*" until she died. It
even caused our Commandant, Nasonov, pity, and he went somewhere
in search of some milk. He said that he knew a *sivieranka* who had a
cow, and from whom he could bring a little milk, perhaps even enough
to save the child's life. In two days' time he returned with milk, but
unfortunately it was already too late. Alinka died, in the arms of her
mother, with the word *mlimli* on her burning, dying lips.

It was the first death in our family – and what a tragedy it was.
Wujek himself made the coffin out of unpolished, rough-hewn planks
of pine. Her tiny body was put into this crude coffin, and my uncle and
my brother Zdzichu pulled her to the cemetery on sledges. Those of us
who had some clothes to put on, followed them, dragging our knees
through the snow. My auntie fainted when they lowered the coffin
through the hole, dug in the frozen soil. On this grave my uncle laid
a cross, made of white pine wood.

When spring eventually came, we children explored the forest,
and the first thing we stumbled on was the cemetery. There were
already a great number of collapsed graves bearing Russian Orthodox
crosses, and we also spotted Catholic crosses on the graves of earlier
Polish political exiles. When we came across Alinka's grave we saw

that apart from the white pine cross, on the grave of Alinka stood a figure of Mary, mother of God, with the child Jesus in her arms. Some good person, who obviously lamented this loss of a young child, who had been deprived unlawfully of her life, had put this statue here. We never found out who it was.

The death of Alinka left a deep mark on my soul. She often came to me in dreams and visions. And to this day I can still hear her whispering, "*mlimli, mlimli, mlimli...*"

Work allocation

The adult men were sent to other camps, particularly Lesopunkt – which was a forestry-specific labour camp – by the river Yezhuga.[2] During the winter they would cut down giant trees, and in spring they sent them downriver. Youngsters from age 16 were separated from their families and sent to different forestry labour camps. My sister Zosia was sent to the labour camp called Trofimo, somewhere far from us, and my brother Zdzichu was sent to Temnaia (literally, "dark"), not too far from us. These camps were gulags for young people who either had to cut down trees, dig up stumps, or harvest the grass from overgrown lakes, and dry it as hay for horses.

They left myself and Tadek with our mother as we were small children, and mum had to work hard and earn money for our upkeep. Mum knew how to read and write well in Russian, because when Poland had been occupied by Czars she had been forced to learn the language at school – now it was a great help. Thanks to her knowledge of Russian, she was appointed to be a cook. She also had to know how to count, which helped her calculate how much food was needed for

---

[2] A feeder river of the Pinega river.

however many people there were without making a mistake – because if you did you would be punished immediately.

Mum was a very good cook, and she made macaroni, which was sprinkled with sugar or covered with oil and given as a second dish. Fish, caught from local lakes, was a frequent main course. Mostly they were roach and perch, which you had to clean first. I often came to help the cleaning of these fish; Commandant Nasonov was a good person, and did not object. For me this was a great joy, because I could eat as much as I wanted, and moreover could bring home some food for my hungry cousins and my little brother. I brought home sugar and raw pastry, which mum had made. The sugar was in big chunks, and you had to hit it with an axe to get reasonable size pieces, and I always managed to smuggle a little of it through. Mum turned the pastry into sheets and wrapped it round my waist so nobody would notice.

I didn't like the taste of the fish, because it was fried in whale fat, which was very smelly, but there wasn't any other oil. The main dish we got was fish soup – but the soup which mum made was very tasty, not like the ones with which they had fed us at the stops on the journey, bobbing with eyeballs. So it was wonderful when mum worked in the kitchen. Unfortunately, all the good times ended when we were moved to another camp, Kołos.

***

In the meantime, Zosia had been sent to another labour camp, Gryfino; here are her words about her experience:

"They formed us into brigades and appointed brigade leaders, one of whom was from among their people, someone who knew forestry work. Some brigades were sent to the forests to chop trees, others to carry the logs to a particular drop-off point. Women who had never held saws or axes in their hands had to chop branches from the felled trees, pile them up and burn them – but it was winter after all. Frost bit our noses. Snow mounted up to our waists: it was hard to move, let alone work. After a day of this work it was impossible to move either an arm or a leg, they were so stiff.

"The elderly sawed firewood for the communal kitchen and to fuel the smoky stoves in their own houses. In spring the temperature began to rise. Huge, heavy and very wet hats of snow fell from the trees as the snow rapidly began to melt. Now one had to walk up to one's knees in wet, melting snow along the forest path – you could hardly make it back home. Your legs were frozen, soaked in shoes made of pigs' skin, which hurt and itched mercilessly. I couldn't sleep, I cried all night. There was nowhere to dry your shoes or clothes properly, so in the morning you had to put them on again wet, and go to work in order to make enough money for food, and to pay for padded jackets and pig-skin shoes. (These were the worst, cheapest ones, but you still had to pay for them.)

"We didn't have any experience in forestry work – we were not lumberjacks – so we didn't earn very much, and we never had enough money to get credit. Hunger squeezed you like a belt around your waist.

"When spring came the snows melted; broken ice began to move on the river, and water ran clear from the ice floes. Then began the log-floating. It was a heavy and dangerous operation. One had to walk over the logs, pushing them and separating them with crooks in order to prevent them clumping together in big piles, so they wouldn't dam up the river. The Russian Brigadier was overseeing this operation, giving instructions, while in the floating barges they cooked meals in canteens. Mostly it was fish soup and half a kilo of bread for lunch. We could smell the soup from a distance, so we lost our appetite, but hunger always overcame the aversion. When the float was finished, we would return to the forest, and so on, and so on."

***

In Camp Głuboki, there was a stable, and in its attic lay a tall heap of children's shoes. Many children had evidently died here from among the exiled people who had lived here in the past, victims of Russian collectivisation. In this camp there were a few unfinished barracks, and one of them was probably going to be a school, except the children had died, so they stopped building it. For us, the children of the community, the building interested us greatly, because we didn't go to school, occupying ourselves instead by exploring the terrain.

One day when they dug a hole to bury rubbish in front of our barrack, they uncovered a large trunk of clothes. There were beautiful embroidered Ukrainian blouses, men's shirts, towels and beautiful multi-coloured scarves and skirts. Everything looked so fresh, as if it had only been put here the day before. But as soon as we touched it, it disintegrated into pieces.

Meeting the Wild Man

Not far from our camp was a lake, where they filled buckets of water to bring to the kitchen. It was boiled and called "*kipiatok*", which anyone could take for free in the morning for breakfast, or for supper in the evening. We used to go to this lake in the summer to bathe. My brother

Zdzichu swam across the whole lake, right to the other side; he sat there for a while, rested, then swam back. He was an excellent swimmer. Tadzio and I, on the other hand, didn't yet know how to swim, so we made ourselves floats from reeds, and taught ourselves to swim with them. This is how we made the floats: we bound the reed stalks with string, then tied two of these branches together so that we lay on the string and the floats were under our arms, and in this way we were able to swim safely. In summer we splashed around there for hours, until we got abscesses in our armpits, neck and anywhere else there were glands. The doctor said it was because we stayed in the water for too long.

While exploring the surroundings we found another two lakes, one not far from the other, divided from each other with a stretch of land. On this land stood a little hut on four stilts, which looked like the hut of "Baba Jaga" – the wicked witch from our children's stories. (Although hers was actually perched on chicken legs.) We were extremely intrigued by this, and naturally wanted to see what was inside. It was hard to get there, because the walls were high for us as children. We stood on each others' shoulders, but this didn't help either. In the end Tadzio called, "Come here, have a look, there's a ladder." And, indeed, in a hole, covered with some wood, was a ladder so we stood it against the hut, and each of us in turn had a look inside. It appeared that someone lived there: one side of the wall was strewn with hay to sleep on, on which was spread a big animal skin; and on the other side lay a pile of crockery, a tin bucket, a little cauldron, dirty on the outside from smoke, and some wooden spoons. We looked around this hut and inside, and were convinced that it was a human who lived here, not an animal. But who could he be? Why did he live here, and not in the camp? Talking about this we headed home.

We began to be a little scared, of wild animals, or of losing the way, and also of the mysterious person who lived in the hut, but fortunately we arrived home. The whole night Tadzio and I couldn't sleep, and the next day we returned with two older boys. We were there as a foursome, chatting happily and loudly, and had almost reached the destination when suddenly, as if from under the ground, appeared before us a huge, terrifying wild man, looking neither human nor animal. He was completely covered with hair, with a white beard almost to his waist, and fixed his wild eyes on us, completely paralysing us with fear; we couldn't move from the spot, or say a thing.

We stood rooted like this, as if we had been struck by lightning. Fortunately he broke the silence with his mumbling. It was hard to understand him. He put his hand on his chest, and we understood this to mean we shouldn't be afraid of him. Then he pointed with his hand at the hut and said, "*moi dom*" – my house. Good, we understood him and our fear began to abate. We replied to him, that "*nasz dom, Polska*" – our home is Poland. He also understood this: "*Aha wi polaki, da*" – ah yes, you are Poles. Our fear disappeared completely, and together we went towards our camp. On the way he turned to the cemetery, and beckoned for us to go with him, so we went. He stood in front of one grave, and we saw that his face was running with thick tears. He showed us five collapsed graves where members of his family were buried, and in front of each he crossed himself.

We, in turn, showed him Alinka's grave, and the other graves marked with white crosses – people from Poland, exiled simply for being Poles, who had died of the winter cold straight after arriving, exhausted by the long journey, the cold and the frost. The man crossed himself with the sign of the crucifix, and said "*O, gospodi, bozhe moi, gospodi pomiluï*" – oh Lord my God, have mercy on them. From this time we became friends, and from time to time he would come to our camp. Commandant Nasanov was kind to him and even let him eat a little in our canteen – he couldn't buy anything for himself because he had no money, but he was much too old to work in the forests. This man told us the whole history of his misfortune during collectivisation in Communist Russia. Suddenly, his visits stopped and we never heard from him again. People said that he was taken to an old peoples' home, or to a kind of prison for old people called "*Deddom*".

Adventure on the lake

Once, Zdzichu, Tadzio and I went to catch fish. We already had "our raft", a craft we'd found by the side of the lake that didn't belong to anybody. Perhaps ten years ago, somebody from one of the early groups of exiles built it. In any case, it was fairly good – the wood was healthy, so we pushed her out onto the lake to catch fish. The best fish were caught in the very early morning. One day we left home very early, before sunrise, and by the time the sun threw its first rays onto the water, we were already happily floating away. It was so quiet: the unspoilt morning peace, murmuring Taiga, and jumping fish plopping around made us sleepy. Our eyes began to close, and standing on the edge of the raft we fell asleep.

Suddenly the silence was broken by Tadzio's shouting – he was splashing in the water, trying to climb onto the raft. He was shouting "Help, save me, my boots are falling off, I can't get onto the raft!" The water was pulling him under the raft, and because it was old its sides were slippery, so he couldn't get a hold. I started to cry, dropped my fishing rod, stretched my hand out to help Tadzio... and I also fell into the water! Fortunately Zdzichu already held Tadzio by his hand; I held onto Tadzio's leg, and so Zdzichu was able to pull us back onto the raft in turn. We were saved, but Tadzio lost one shoe. His hat floated away on the water but Zdzichu managed to catch it with his fishing rod. That's how our fishing trip finished that time: it was lucky that we had learned to swim at least basically with our reed floats, because otherwise it would have ended in tragedy.

Lots of people suffered with "*jazwa*" (abscesses), which were not only a result of staying in the water all the time, but also due to the constant hard work and poor diet. This illness tormented people through the whole time we were in the "Soviet Paradise". The ones on the neck attacked the lymphatic system, and the *jazwa* could develop into tuberculosis of the lymphatic glands. It was a very serious illness which many people suffered, including me. A doctor once had to cut one of my abscesses to make it bleed while we were in the Taiga. It was particularly foul: we had no real bandages, and I'd often find lice feeding on the rags that had been used to stop the bleeding. As I grew older I developed a complex about my neck, always worrying that nobody would love me because of the unsightly scars on my neck. In the end, I had plastic surgery on this *jazwa* scar in England, later in life.

CHAPTER 3 – CAMP KOŁOS

A *lesopunkt* is a labour camp designed for cutting down pine trees on a large scale, and preparing to float them downriver in the spring. The *lesopunkt* where we now arrived was called Kołos, a Russian word with beautiful associations for us, because the similar-sounding *kłos* meant ear of corn in Polish. The word *kołos* awakens the human imagination, and paints beautiful pictures – pictures of fields, "painted with different kinds of grain, as if golden-plated with wheat, and silver-plated with rye" (I allow myself to quote the words of Adam Mickiewicz). Pictures of granaries full of shiny grain; pictures of the meals from the harvest, and of windmills from which the men carry sacks of flour and barley; pictures of ovens, from which emanate the aroma of baked bread; pictures of happiness, contentedness and plenty. But here in Camp Kołos there were none of these things.

Instead, it was made up of a few gloomy barracks for the slave-exiles, and a headquarters for the people in charge – our carers, NKVD-men; next to that was a gaol, and "*kholodnaia*", a very small, freezing room, which fitted one person standing, where they punished people. It was a place for minor offenders (not for the more threatening political plotters): Zosia wasonce put into one of these overnight as punishment for teaching the Polish language to children, so I heard a first-hand account of it. There was also a "*prieomnaia*", a kind of surgery, staffed by just one young lady doctor, who cut out abscesses with an ordinary pen-knife, which she sharpened on a stone. Apart from this knife, aspirin (which was often lacking) and the greasy and black ointment ichthyol, she had nothing else. There was a school there, a stables, canteen, and a nursery – though all were rudimentary.

It was a labour camp situated in a forest by the river Yezhuga, a feeder river to the Pinega. Work here consisted of felling pine trees in the forest, bringing them as logs to the water and floating them downriver. Here you would find neither fields golden with ears of corn, nor collective farms: there were only mighty, impenetrable forests and miserable lumberjacks. I always thought a better name for this would be *Lesorubka* (lumberjackery) than *Kołos*.

Wujek Janek and his family, years after their return. Seated with him is his wife Andzia. Standing from left are Wanda, Ludek, Krysia, her husband Ryszard (not part of the transportation to Siberia) and Balbina.

Kołos was built in a hurry by the strongest men who had previously been sent to Głubokij. In autumn 1940, we were all transported to this new place. This time we were moved by lorries or tractors. The driver of our tractor was a woman, I remember her very well, because it made a great impression on me that a woman was driving. That woman looked and behaved like a man: she was short-built, stocky and red in the face, she was dressed in a padded jacket and padded trousers, and she drove very fast on this bumpy forest track. We were scared that we would be thrown out of the tractor by the continual bumping over roots and holes, but she got us there without any harm. They accommodated us in a very long barrack on each side of which were allocated five families – meaning that all together, ten families were living in one room.

You entered in one door, next to a stove, into a long room, with another stove at the other end, and a passage down the middle of the room, between the beds. Each family had a *nary* (rough bed) made of wooden planks. It was our bed, but also a place to sit. These beds were smaller or bigger depending on how many people were in the family. There were three of us at that time, mum, Tadzio and I, because Zosia and Zdzichu were still in different camps specifically for youths. On our side of the room was Wujek Janek with his family of five, Wujek Ignac with his family of five, one widow, whose son died of hunger shortly after our arrival, and someone else we didn't know so well.

Opposite us, there was Gołębiowski's family – our neighbours from Suszki. Lodzia Gołębiowska had gone to the same primary school as me back in the village. Her mother, Mrs Gołębiowska was a very religious woman, who was always praying and singing religious songs. She had older sons as well as young children, and her lads were very handsome. Over time, these young men disappeared from our camp, never to be heard of again.

***

Autumn suddenly changed into a severe winter. Day and night we had to keep the stove burning. Our windows were covered with a thick layer of frost from the inside, so you had to scrape it away from the glass to let a bit of light in. The temperature reached minus 40°C. As a result of this extreme temperature trees would regularly burst in the Taiga outside, which caused a lot of accidents and fatalities at work. Although the stove was constantly burning, it was nevertheless cold. You had to sleep in your clothes until you warmed up. On top of all this it was very crowded, and there was always an unsavoury smell in the room. Nights were absolute horrors. You couldn't sleep, because either someone was snoring, or crying, or farting or praying out loud, and Mrs Gołębiowski either sang *godzinki* or other religious songs, or she would sit in front of the fire and kill lice in her family's clothes. It was hard to protect yourself from these insects, because of illness, a lack of personal hygiene, a lack of sanitary goods, hunger, overcrowding and the offputting smell. All of this combined to multiply these insects.

Our "carers" were horrified by this situation and asked permission to build bath-houses with special pungent chemical rooms, called "*voshoboiki*", to kill the insects. These were good things in principle. We went to wash ourselves in the baths (*bania*), and our clothes meanwhile went through a debugging process. This cleaning agent didn't last for long, though, because as soon as we came to the barrack, the insects burrowed themselves into our clean clothes even more quickly. They multiplied at an astonishing rate. Unfortunately, it was impossible to put all the people from the barrack through the wash house and insect-room at once. I remember those wash-houses very well; I thought they were a fine invention, even if they didn't exactly work perfectly.

First was a compartment for removing our clothes and putting them into the stove for processing. Naked, you went through into the next room in which heated stones glowed hot from the burning wood beneath them, like a stove, and there were three benches along the sides. You poured water over the stones creating hot steam, which carried up, so that those who wanted to heat themselves up lay on the highest bench. In this wash-house women and children went through together. Russian women brought *"wieniki"* with them – little bunches made of birch tree twigs, and beat themselves and each other with them. This "massage" helped stimulate the blood circulation. After the steaming process we went to a different room, where there were wooden bowls, and water in barrels, one cold, one hot, and here we washed ourselves. After this process, a person felt new-born.

Drying room between barracks

Between our barrack and the other was the so-called drying room, where workers, when they came home, dried their clothes and shoes. This place was always warm, but very, very smelly, and the worst thing about it was that all the insects were incubated there – lice, fleas, cockroaches and bed-bugs all together. Because of the stench and the insects the authorities didn't care to look into this room. That is why this place was used for political or religious meetings. Our carers, NKVD-men, took great pains to make sure we did not get any news from the outside world, and they kept us under strict control. The Commandant of this camp was called Wisniakow, a military man and a great Communist. Every evening he came with a list and read our names aloud in a roll-call by first name, second name and patronymic, and we had to present ourselves to him. During the day he inspected the barracks, ordering us to take down pictures of saints and religious paraphernalia from the walls. Belief in God was mocked. In school, crosses or religious medallions were torn away from children's necks and thrown through the window. The NKVD-men worked hardest to try to convert the children into Communists. They checked the barracks and mocked God, but they never checked the drying rooms, and that's where we had our meetings.

A certain old lady, Soszyńska, carried out religious services. We prayed together and we sang religious songs, which kept people from death and kept our spirits alive, giving us strength to live. Also in attendance there were men who brought interesting news from the outside world about war and politics. The drying rooms, which were incubators for all kinds of insects, also turned into incubators of our hope and strength for survival.

School

As I already mentioned, there was a school in this labour camp. We had two teachers, a man and a woman, who was called Milańja Wasiliewna. They put Tadzio and me into the second grade, although in Poland we were already going into the fourth grade. They did this because we had to learn the Russian tongue before anything else. They taught us a great number of songs and poems by heart, which I remember to this day. We went to this school reluctantly; the teachers mocked God, and didn't allow us to bear crucifixes or medallions on our necks. Once, in my class, the teacher approached a nine-year-old boy called Benek, tore a medallion from his neck and threw it through the window. Benek didn't think twice, but immediately took off one of his rubber boots and threw it at the teacher.

Such behaviour was not tolerated: the teacher called him a hooligan and called the militia. They took him away, and we never saw him again. He was put into a young offenders' prison. Poor Benek! I remember him well, because we used to play together. He was half-orphaned like I was. The difference was that his mother had died just after arriving to Kołos, while we were already exiled as half-orphans, without our father. For Benek it was a great tragedy to have his medallion removed. First they had deprived him of his country, then his mother and now his God. And in the end, they deprived him of his father's care, and completely of his freedom. These kinds of occurrence were very frequent.

In the new year of 1941, they organised a "*jołka*" for us – a Christmas-tree celebration (that is, a new year celebration with a decorated tree – emphatically NOT Christmas). The tree was decorated with different chains which we made ourselves from coloured paper, or different toys, like locomotives, tractors, sickles and hammers. Next to the *jołka* stood a Father Christmas replacement – *Dzied Moroz*, or Old Man Frost – and "*Snieguroczka*", a beautiful Snow Girl who accompanied him. The teacher said: "Well, children, pray to your God and ask for presents." There was quiet while everybody whispered something to themselves... and nothing happened. "Now," the teacher said, "and now pray to Uncle Stalin." Again there was a silence, which was broken by the opening door. All eyes turned to the doorway, and –

oh wonder! – two soldiers came in with a huge basket full of presents. They put the basket in front of the tree, and walked out again. "Now," said the teacher, "you see children, your God gave you nothing, your God is weak and doesn't care about you. Well, but Uncle Stalin is good, and strong, he can do everything! He loves children, and you just have to ask him and you will have everything!"

After the New Year, we very often missed lessons, and if somebody warned us that the militia men were looking for schoolchildren, then we hid under our bed. But once he found us, threatening us with his gun, and shouted: "Come out, or I will kill you like dogs." These are my memories from my school in Kołos.

The work and subsistence effort of Camp Kołos

Compared with our life at Camp Głubokij, our fortune now changed for the worse. At Głubokij mum had worked as a cook, so we always had something to eat – but there was already a cook at Kołos. The cook, along with all the kitchen staff, belonged to the first pioneers who came here to build a new labour camp by the shores of the River Yezhuga. Since they were the primary inhabitants, they had employment priority. If they were not guilty of any wrongdoing there was no reason to make them redundant and take on somebody else at the kitchen. So instead, mum was appointed to forestry work.

Those people assigned to cutting down pine trees were called *lesoruby* (lumberjacks) and those moving the logs with horses, were called *vozchiki* – transporters. Those who threw logs down to the river from the pile were called *splavchiki* – floaters. They gave mum a horse, called Waśka; and so, from being a cook, she became a *vozchik*. My Ciocia Andzia (my godmother) didn't know how to handle a horse, so she was appointed to chop branches from fallen pine trees, put them on a pile and burn them.

My sister was a *lesorub*, and she told us about her and other peoples' work, and how they did it. First, *lesorubi* had to remove snow from around the pine tree in order to make its base accessible: the snow was sometimes a metre or two high. They chopped open an aperture with axes and then, using a saw, two people would cut through it.

When the pine tree toppled, another group of people had to dig it out from the deep snow, chop off the branches and cut the trunks into logs with specific measurements. They dragged them into a collecting area, where *voschiki* came with their sledges and loaded up the logs. The sledges were called *volokusche*, distinguished from normal sledges because they were very low so the logs could be loaded on. Some of them were tied on the front of the sledge and the rest were pulled along behind. The workers dragged their cargo to the riverbank where the logs were unloaded. On the riverbank men stacked them into piles again, where they waited for springtime, and their journey downriver.

The work in the forests was very heavy, hard and dangerous. There were often severe accidents, even deaths. I remember when a young woman, previously a teacher, was crushed by the branches of a falling pine tree, and before they were able to clear the branches and reach her she was already dead. I will never forget saying farewell to her. She was lying in a coffin in the barracks dressed in a very beautiful blue dress, and she wore a white shawl on her head. She looked as if she was alive. She had two young children who we could not tear away from the coffin, they were crying so badly. In comparison with forestry work, my mum preferred to work with her horse carrying logs to the river from the forest. My mum liked animals and she managed well with the horse, although it was as stubborn as an ass. She shared her problems with this horse, and sometimes her food, even though we suffered a frightful hunger.

My mother (left) as a young woman, with a friend.

Waśka – my mother's horse

In the Taiga horses were very valuable, more so than people. The horse was considered a Soviet worker, and a human being was just a meaningless exile, a galley slave. Therefore the slave had to take great care of his horse because if anything happened to it, it was your fault, and you would be better off dead. My mum had to be very resourceful in her dealings with Waśka, as the following story shows.

For no discernable reason, Waśka refused to work one day. For no price would he move from the spot with his load. It was winter, and it was getting dark. The frost was becoming more and more severe every minute as night fell. If the horse didn't pull then a white death was inevitable. The men tried to help mum, whipping him and making a clamour. But whatever they did, Waśka wouldn't take a step. He stood like a rock, and nothing bothered him – had they been about to kill him he would not have moved. The horse had obviously also had enough of the slavework in the forest!

The men, seeing they would not win with the horse tried to persuade my mum to leave the stubborn beast in the forest and come home with them. But mum couldn't abandon the horse because if something happened to it, she would be severely punished, perhaps imprisoned. She was, of course, also scared to stay in the forest alone, because at this time of year she would not survive through to the morning because of the cold; and there was also the threat of wolves. The men left my mum, and she stayed with the horse, alone, face to face. She didn't know what to do, so she embraced the horse by the neck and started to cry on his neck. She cried and begged the horse very gently, as gently as she could: "*Vasia, Vasen'ka, tiani*" – little Waśka, my dear little Waśka, please pull. It's hard to believe, but this animal seemed to understand the pleading of a despairing woman, and suddenly moved on. He snorted and pawed the ground with his hooves into the frozen snow. Waśka moved forward so quickly that my mum hardly managed to run fast enough to keep up with him.

Obviously, he wanted to catch up on the time he had lost, and reach the river before nightfall – and he managed it! There were still people who had not arrived home when Waśka, sweating, proudly snorted, and stood with his load at the appointed place. Mum patted and stroked her dear horse, and said *"spasibo, Vasen'ka, spasibo"* – thank you, dearest Waśka, thank you. Those who had still not left for home helped my mum unload the logs from the sledge, and they continued home together.

It was already dark when mum reached our barrack. She was very tired, but pleased. My brother and I had begun to worry about our mum because she had not come home for so long, but when she told us the story of Waśka we were overjoyed that it had ended so well. We were proud of mum and Waśka, and we admired him for being such a clever and good horse. I loved him anyway – partly because mum used to take food from his bag for us, so that he fed us too, in his way. The next day we gave him our ration of sugar as a reward for saving our mother's life.

Illnesses and diseases

As I mentioned above, my mother sometimes took a little bit of food from the horse and brought it home for us, but she couldn't do it often, in case the horse got too weak and died. When she was first given this horse the foreman had told her: *"Khrani etu loshad', a to, esli loshad' podokhnet to i ty podokhnesh*" – look after this horse well, because if the horse dies you will die too.

On the riverbank stood a *kipiatiłka* – a large shed in which was a big cauldron filled with water from the river. One person was responsible for this *kipiatiłka*, and looked after it so that from earliest morning to latest night, water was constantly on the boil. I have previously mentioned that this water was known as *kipiatok*, but it's useful to stress again how important it was to us. It was the only food (not that it was much good as food) that you could have for free, and you could have as much as you wanted, as often as you wanted. So, we would crush our bread in a bowl, and pour the boiling water over it; it was our main daily meal throughout a very long winter which lasted from the end of September until May. Sometimes mum managed to exchange some clothes for food with Russian women who were foremen, or tractor drivers, and who lived in the region permanently. But it happened very rarely.

There was a terrible starvation, strong frost, short days and long, dark nights. People suffered terribly, and were psychologically destroyed. They had no hope of surviving and lost their will to live. Poor children had neither a drop of milk, or butter, or lard, or potatoes or any other vegetables: there was nothing. There was nothing. Bread was rationed to 800g per day per working person, and 200g for children and for those who were not qualified for work, the so-called *izhdiventsy*. These included the unqualified, ill, elderly, and invalids, all suffering this policy: *kto ne rabotaet, ne kushaet* – he who doesn't work, doesn't eat.

There was a canteen and you could buy yourself portions of soup or barley-porridge, but it cost a lot and there was not enough money left from what mum earned. The workers had food brought to them in the forests, but they had to pay for these portions. They deducted this debt on their pay-day. For the rest of the money that mum had left after deductions, we bought bread rations for Tadek and me, and from time to time we could buy one portion of soup or porridge for the two of us to share. When mum reached the required norm at work, then she received an additional payment known as *Stakhanovka* – that is, according to the level set by Stakhanov (the equivalent for men was called *Stakhanovets*). And then we could buy a little bit more bread, but it cost a huge amount; if it was more than your ration you had to pay four or five times more.

People started to become terribly ill. Apart from abscesses, there was water retention, they started to get scurvy, their teeth fell out (my sister once pulled one out then pushed it back in again), and they developed chicken blindness so they could not see at night. Chicken blindness was probably the worst and most dangerous illness, because when it started to become dark, those sufferers would become completely lost. They couldn't find their way home; they stumbled, fell, hit their heads. The worst scenario was when they didn't return from the forests before dark – especially when they had become separated from their group. Then it was the end of their lives. They couldn't see the road, they collapsed into snow, and the "white death" consumed them forever. There were many cases of the white death. The camp doctor was hopeless. The only medicine which she prescribed was the eating of liver. For liver you had to wait until an old horse died. Then people went to the butcher with their prescription, and they got this miracle cure.

In spring and summer it was a little better. People took themselves to the woods to get food. Snow still lay on the ground, but mushrooms which we called *murlhle* began to show their brown crumpled heads through the snow. They were edible, but you have to know how to cook them. In my case, after eating these mushrooms I almost lost my life. I was terribly poisoned; I was in convulsions, and nothing helped me, neither castor oil given as a purgative, nor any herbal teas which the women boiled up for me.

Mrs Soszińska, the lady who prayed to God in the drying areas of our home, brought me some holy water, and she asked me to drink it. It still didn't help me, but my Wujek Ignac brought two potatoes and a glass of milk. God knows where he took it from, because up to that day I hadn't seen a drop of milk or a single potato. By the time he brought this glass of milk it had already gone sour, so he must have brought it a great distance. I don't know whether it was the praying, the holy water or the milk – or the potato – but something helped me, and I didn't die.

Spring was now in full bloom. My mum took me outside and sat on the bench in front of the barrack. The spring air smelt wonderful, like a new life. The sun was lovely and warm. I didn't have any more pain. I wanted to live, although my life was so hard. I was still only 13 years old.

Adventures in the forest: the bear

After my recovery, my brother Tadek and I set off into the forest to forage for food. That spring was full of charm and beauty. The sun was warming the earth, and the snow melted all of a sudden. The entirety of the Taiga's nature burst into life. Sorrel leaves appeared in clearings, pushing up among nettles. On the overgrown, marshy lakes cranberries started to appear, full of vitamin C... even if they were still frozen. We gathered what we could, sorrel leaves and nettles, taking it home to cook, which satisfied our hunger somewhat. Slightly later in the season, wild strawberries could be found on the riverbanks, which my brother and I went out for. And at about that time we came across something we hadn't bargained for.

On one of these foraging missions we were sitting quietly like little birds, picking these aromatic berries – putting some into our baskets, but putting many others straight into our mouths. We weren't paying any attention to our surroundings. We had almost collected a full basket of these berries, when suddenly we heard a noise, a grunting-growling, and then a loud splash of water. Jumping to our feet, we almost died from fear – a huge brown bear was swimming across the river in our direction. We started to run; at first we had to make the climb up the wet bank, but our feet were paralysed with fear, so we kept falling down. At last we managed to reach dry land and the path which led to our camp. We sprinted as if the devil was on our heels, as they say, throwing away our berry baskets to distract the bear, since they like sweet berries very much.

We were scared and pale when we reached home. Perhaps this *mishka* had not been interested in us, but how were we supposed to know that? This adventure didn't deter us from returning to the forest, I should say. Through the short summer we had to fortify ourselves, and the forest gave us essential food; everything grew so quickly and ripe. A multiplicity of edible mushrooms sprang up, the best mushroom you can get, boletus, ceps and *kozlaki* of many different colours and sizes, plus *borówki*, rare red berries. There were *ridz* mushrooms of two kinds, too: one, like our Polish variety, orange; the other grew in autumn, and had a beige colour. We called them Soviet *ridz*; the Russians salted them in barrels for winter.

Adventures in the forest: our night in the Taiga

Later the same summer, my mother, Tadek and I returned to the forest to pick berries and gather mushrooms. It was early evening, after mum came home from work. She said: "Children let's go to the forest, to get some berries for supper." We set off, carrying baskets for mushrooms and cans for berries. At first we sensibly walked near the path, and didn't enter the deep forest, but we couldn't find any of the food we were looking for. Evidently, other people had got there before us. Gradually we started to search ever more deeply into the forest. Enormous bushes of bilberries began to appear, completely untouched. We set to picking them hurriedly, and filled both our hungry stomachs and our empty containers.

There were further treats on the forest floor. The red caps of fantastic mushrooms called *kraśnuki* emerged. These mushrooms are very healthy and very tasty (they look like *prawdziwki* (boletus), their hats red from the top, the underbelly a white-yellow). They had very hard and thick stems, higher than boletus. I had never seen these mushrooms in Poland. We were enchanted by this miracle of nature's fecundity, and having filled our cans with berries, we started on the mushrooms. Each specimen was better than the last, more beautiful and aromatic than the last; as if in sympathy, the forest was humming mysteriously and inviting us into its depths: "Come further, there are more surprises waiting for you."

As if hypnotised, we pushed into the depths of the Taiga, ever further from our path. When the containers were full of berries and mushrooms we stopped, and enjoyed the satisfaction of our expedition. But then our joy turned into a nightmare. Regaining composure, we emerged from under the spell and returned to reason: suddenly we understood the situation we were in. The forest had completely changed its nature – it was incredibly dense and very, very dark, and the humming had become threatening, as if to give us a signal of approaching danger.

Tadek and I with our mother, shortly after my father died.

We could hear a multitude of mysterious voices belonging to the Taiga. They all seemed to be telling us, "Flee, run away as quickly as you can." Suddenly an enormous bird flapped his wings and with a terrible shrieking flew up; after him shot up one after another. This utterly terrified my brother and I and we began to beg mum to take us back. She wasn't ready to yet, but said, "OK, OK children, let's go." However, whichever way we faced imposing forest blocked our path. It looked different from its normal appearance, so thick, so black. We ran after our mum, but kept tripping over. We had to cross a pile of pine trees that had been toppled by the wind; we couldn't, and we slipped.

Near Russia's Polar Circle, in the Taiga, there are often winds – perhaps they come from the Arctic Ocean – so strong that enormous pine trees are torn up with their roots, one on top of another. You had to go round these windfalls for up to a mile at a time, because you simply couldn't climb them. I remember my mum was very frightened. She dashed to one side then to the other; we knew that we had lost our way in the impenetrable, dangerous Taiga.

As dusk fell, mosquitoes and little midges (known as *moszka* in Russian), bit us mercilessly. Unable to guard against these awful insects our eyes swelled from the bites and we couldn't see where we were going. We were in a state of despair, not knowing what to do, or which direction to head in. Tadek climbed the tallest pine tree he could find in the hope of catching any sign of life with which we could orientate ourselves. He shouted from the top of the tree with all his might, and we shouted too, but nobody heard us.

So we walked and walked – completely disorientated. Meanwhile it was getting ever darker, and the Taiga was humming more threateningly. Then all of a sudden, the view before us was a little lighter, heralding a clearing, filled with many huge haystacks. Standing by one of these haystacks was a big animal. Because it was quite dark we couldn't recognise what sort of animal it was; Tadek and I thought it was a horse. Mum realised that she recognised the area we'd stumbled on – she had once scythed grassed for the horses here. Approaching cautiously, we noticed the animal had big horns, and when it saw us, it jumped, startled, and fled into the forest. Mum told us that it was a reindeer, so we shouldn't be afraid of it, if it returned to eat the hay, because reindeers, though they live in the wild, don't do any harm to humans. However, whether or not it was a reindeer, to this day I am not convinced.

Now it was completely dark, and although mum had realised where we were, it was folly to walk the Taiga after dark, because you could drown in those marshes covered with grass and moss. It had happened many times: many people had gone to pick cranberries and Siberian raspberries and had never come back. There was no other option, we had to stay in one of the stacks overnight. We made a big hole in the side of one of them, into which we climbed and remained overnight. For a long time I couldn't fall asleep; although I wasn't scared of the reindeer, there were many other animals like wolves and bears in the forest that I was quite rightly afraid of. So, full of fear, we stayed there till the morning, when we set off home safely.

Summer passed quickly – too quickly – and as time passed many changes came in politics and in our lives.

CHAPTER 4 – FROM THE DIARY OF MY SISTER ZOSIA

Division of work

> 1) *Rabotchij* class of worker, the first class of worker. The strongest people, "working class", the hardest working teams. They were men and youths from 16, they were qualified to chop trees, carry logs to the banks of the river and float them in spring.
> 2) Women were qualified to chop branches from fallen pine trees, put the branches on a pile and burn them.
> 3) The elderly were qualified to saw wood for firewood for the kitchen and for heating the stoves in the barracks.

All these kinds of work were just like slavery. In spring the big snowdrifts melted and there was a lot of flooding. You had to walk up to your knees in this melting snow. Those who walked in the forests all day had wet feet from morning till evening, all the time. They had pig-skin shoes, and the snow and water which melted inside was slopping around the whole time. When people came home after work, they hardly managed to stand on their feet, which were red from the snow and cold water. And at night they were aching and itching so much that you couldn't sleep. All night we cried from pain. There was not any medicine, not even aspirin. The pig-skin shoes were very cold. They did not dry overnight. There was no room for all the shoes to be left out to dry, but in the morning you had to put them on half wet, and go again to the forest to work, to reach the norm [of productivity] in order to get money to pay for shoes, and padded jackets and for trousers, and for 80g of bread and some soup.

And if you didn't make the norm levels, the payment was very little, virtually nothing. It took a long time before Polish people learnt to work in the forest and reach the norm. In spring they took us to the work of floating the logs on the river. Floating work was organised but very dangerous. This field of work was supervised by an experienced Russian foreman. One had to walk across the floating logs and push them around with an iron hook as the foreman instructed. It was easy to slip, fall in the water and be crushed by the power and speed of the floating logs. You had to be very careful and nimble. There were sheds where food was prepared, soup made from dried fish with an especially sharp smell. Local workers, natives, loved this soup and ate their fill of it. For the Poles, the very smell killed the appetite – but hunger will make a human being accustom himself to anything.

The Russians laughed at us, and used to say *"priviknietie"* – you will get used to it. And it was true, I got used to this smell, and the soup was in fact very tasty. There were other meals, like soup from green tomatoes, soup from oats (*ovsianka*, rough with lots of fibre), *kasza* with a drop of oil and always half a kilo of bread. On the floating shift they fed us well. We were considered as first class workers. And it was the truth, that *"kto rabotaet, tot kushaet, a kto ne rabotaet, ne kushaet"* – he who works, eats, and he who doesn't work, doesn't eat.

Conditions were different back in the camps. There, people hungered and sickened horribly – scurvy, tuberculosis, typhus, chicken blindness, water retention born of starvation. There were no doctors. People treated themselves with birch tree juice, and tea with fresh pine tree buds. Not a single drop of milk, or a single potato could be found, even with the brightest candle. In the labour camps there were neither cows, nor chickens; native villages were 100km away from each other, and no-one knew anything about them. After two months work at the wood floating area, we returned to our bug-infested camps, where our families lived, and again were set to work in the forest, chopping down the pine trees, and sawing logs to the special measurements, and putting these chopped logs into special arrangements as demanded. The saws were sharpened by a native expert called a *pilostav*, but our people sharpened the axes. The axes were huge and heavy. It was monotonous and hard work, and drove you mad.

Every day, returning home after work, one would hear that someone or other had died. The despair of families was all around, children wailing, ill people crying. Dead bodies lay along corridors until funerals were organised. The sight was horrifying: you would walk into the barrack and you could see in the corridor on a bed of planks, swollen or dried up skin, the shrivelled remains of family members. Children gathered, weeping after their mummy or daddy

Zosia and I in 1947.

who would no longer heed their cries. Slowly a person accustomed himself to the sight of dying people, or dead bodies, and resigned himself to the fate that it could happen to him tomorrow.

Hunger, illness and death were the companions of us convicts, deprived of humanity. The number of living decreased, the number of dead increased. These people moved from the barrack to behind the barracks, in the forest, this time not to work, but to go to their everlasting rest. Behind our camp somewhere on a little hill, the graves of our people were multiplying, adult graves, and children's graves.

In July 1941, we received information that our lot may soon be improving. Our young men began to disappear; others were bringing information that Hitler had cheated Stalin. They said that Hitler's army, without declaring war, had invaded the Soviet Union. Our "carers" had meetings, after which they changed their attitude to us for the better. They began to treat us as humans, and not like dogs. In the end, they told us that there was war with Germany, that on 22 July 1941, Hitler's Germans had eventually admitted their duplicity and declared war. For us it had been the best news since the moment of our exile. There was news of our liberation! It was almost a miracle. All the Poles were delighted with the war, since it opened up the road to our freedom, and the return to our motherland – POLAND.

CHAPTER 5 – AMNESTY, SUMMER 1941: GENERAL ANDERS' ARMY

On 31 July 1941, in London, a treaty was concluded between Poland and the Soviet Union to return to diplomatic relations, and to give each other support and help in the war against Hitler's Germany. A Polish army in the Soviet Union was to be established. A protocol was added to this treaty about an amnesty for all exiled Poles in the Soviet Union. This treaty was signed by General Sikorski and Stalin in Moscow. In the Polish–Soviet Treaty, from the end of July, the Russian side agreed to the formation of a Polish Army on Russian territory. The formation of the army began immediately in August 1941. Władysław Anders, General of the Polish division, was appointed to the charge of the Polish Army in the Soviet Union, whose evacuation from Russia to Iran took place from 9 August 1942.

The organisation of the Polish army took place in the more civilised territory of the Soviet Union, near ports and towns, not in the middle of the impenetrable forests. People who were cast into the depths of the Taiga, 100km or more from a railway or river port, found out about it only after a great delay. At last we began to be told that we were now free, that our presence would not be checked every day, and that we could determine our own movements around the Archangel region. But we had to do it on our own initiative – there would be no help from the authorities – calculating our own plans to escape from this dark place and return to humanity. Our carers tried to persuade us not to go anywhere, but to stay put until the war was finished. They told us that this was a safe place, that the Germans would not come here, and that when everything returned to normal they would take us back themselves.

They wanted the Poles to obtain Russian citizenship, and sign work contracts (which meant we would be paid more), and then, if we wanted, we could even build our own houses: they would give us cows and chickens, "*i budet khorosho!*" – and all will be good! But nobody believed them. Each individual, each family, wanted to run away from this hole, towards civilisation, and, most of all, to Poland.

Zosia and Zdzichu, who had been living in a different camps, now joined us. My brother had turned 17 in January, and my sister was not yet 20. Now our family was complete, and we began to prepare ourselves for the journey. But we Poles faced a difficult task: how to get out of here? There was neither road nor transport. What to do? How to do it? We gathered and disputed, and came up with an inventive solution: rafts. On a raft, the river would carry us to a bigger river. At these rivers we might find steamships, and on these we could sail further and yet further – as far as possible from this hell, "where the Devil says goodnight".

On a raft on the river Pinega

Wujek Janek, Zdzichu and other Poles started to build river-going rafts. Ours was made of 20 logs, tied incredibly tightly using long vines from trees so they wouldn't fall apart. During our journey down the river, they added another two logs on each side because under our weight we were taking on too much water. It actually looked quite comfy: we even had a tented area which protected us and our belongings from the rain. At the beginning, in one corner, was a stove made from clay, where we had a fire lit and cooked food. Our raft was one of the larger ones – big enough to fit two families on it, Janek's five and our five. So, in total, there were ten individuals plus all our belongings! I don't remember exactly but somewhere at the end of August we boarded the raft and set off into unknown territory. Other Poles did the same; no-one knew anything, whether we were doing the right thing, how far we had to go in order to reach some kind of landing bay, what the river would be like and whether it would carry us safely. No-one even allowed themselves to consider the danger. Just one wish dominated every Pole's mind: to escape, to escape from this place, and as quickly as possible.

The Yezhuga was not a regulated river: it presented all sorts of new horrors. It was full of currents, whirlpools, rocks and rapids. However, people thought that if the river was good enough to float commercial logs down, it must be good enough to carry people. So we floated along. Wujek Janek, with my brother and sister, had long poles and stood at the sides taking care of our direction, ensuring that the raft didn't run into any problems. My mother and aunt looked after the fire, while we children sat in the tented area, or in the middle of the raft, or we tried to sleep. Of the children, I was the oldest at 13, but I was very small and thin. Tadek was 11, and was also a very small boy; my aunt's three daughters, Krysia, Wanda and Balbina, were even younger and smaller, 10, 8 and 4 years old.

My sister says that the younger children were afraid, and cried with fear. Indeed, there often was something to fear – especially when the raft would fall into a whirlpool, or get stuck on an underwater rock and have to be pushed loose. Once we hit one of these rocks and were left spinning 360 degrees, our luggage and cooking equipment hurled into the waters. We just couldn't get loose, until Zdzichu got off the raft into the water and used a metal bar to dislodge it. The whirlpool shot the raft away leaving my brother in the middle of the river; the metal bar was really heavy and my brother, an èxcellent swimmer, had trouble staying afloat. We managed to get to the side of the river and wait for him – it was an awful ordeal, and we thought there was no way he would make it. It would have been easier without the metal bar, but he couldn't bring himself to lose such an important tool. The next time we had to do this, they tied my brother with a rope so that they could tow him back in after the raft was free.

It was now September, getting dark earlier, and the evenings and nights were bitterly cold. We only floated during the day, and at night we tied the raft to the river bank, where we would go into the forest, find dry wood and make a fire. From time to time we would come across a fisherman's hut where we would spend the night. Sometimes we would see a village, where people spoke Russian but looked very different from our NKVD guards or our teachers and doctor in the camp. They were shorter and more squat, and had red cheeks on prominent cheekbones. They called themselves *Sivieranie*. They were very good and kind people. When we had the good fortune to meet a village like this, Zdzichu, Zosia and Janek would stay overnight to look after the raft, while my mother, aunt and the five children would go into the village begging them to take us for the night. These people never chased us away; they always took us into their homes; they always sat us at their table with the family, and shared their own food with us.

That was the first time I saw a real Russian *samovar*, from which our host poured *kipiatok*, not to a glass but into saucers, and gave us slices of dried bread (*suchari*) and told us to dip them into the water and eat. We even found baked potatoes on the table sometimes, with mushrooms pickled in brine as accompaniment. These mushrooms were called *"wolnuchi"*, similar to Polish *ridz*, except that they gave off a white, bitter milk when you cut them, whereas with *ridz* the milk is orange and not bitter. In autumn the whole Taiga is covered in these mushrooms; people gather them in baskets and salt them in wooden barrels for winter. The salt and ice neutralise their poison, and they were beyond delicious. The *Sivieranie* didn't just feed us, they put us up. They gave us the best places to sleep, on top of the stove – a privileged spot in the house, where elderly grandparents and young children were usually allowed to sleep to keep warm. It turned out that *Sivieranie* had European features – they were victims of the mass exile of stubborn, rich landowners who refused to "join collectivisation" between 1929 and 1933.

When we didn't find a village we had to sleep on the bank of the river. Someone had to look after the raft – not because someone would steal it, but in case it came loose and floated away. On one occasion, Zdzichu stayed on board while the rest of us went to collect dry branches and twigs for the campfire. We had to get lots of this, because the nights were long and very, very cold. When the fire was prepared, the younger children were put to sleep, and the rest of us sat up and talked. Suddenly, we heard footsteps cracking dry twigs, and howling nearby. Zosia quickly assured us it must be dogs – that it certainly wasn't dangerous.

We had to put lots of wood on the fire and they wouldn't come because they would be afraid of it. In the morning a fisherman told us that they hadn't been dogs after all, but wolves! That they infested the forests all around, and that we had been extremely lucky not to have been attacked. Zosia, of course, had known full well they were wolves not dogs, but hadn't wanted to scare us. She knew that as long as the fire was burning they would be too scared to come close. She later told me that when she'd been collecting sticks she'd heard them pawing after her nearby.

We flowed along the Yezhuga for a week or two, I don't remember – but it felt like a very long time, especially as the temperature kept dropping, and occasional drifts of snow would descend. We were worried that winter would fall while we were still on the raft, especially since we had no idea how much longer we had to be on it. Suddenly one day, a giant body of water opened in front of us. To us children, it seemed like it was the *sea*! We were terrified at the prospect. It turned out that this was the mouth of the Yezhuga as it joined the River Pinega. On this larger river lies a small port, from which steamers left for the northern River Dwina. From here you could go right up to Archangel, the giant port on the White Sea, or to the left down to Kotlas, where Polish people were gathering for mass transportation, joining the army and their family. Here lay the doorway to the south of Russia, and beyond that Iran – in other words, it raised the prospect of leaving Russia!

The "big body of water" caused huge trouble to the rafting Poles. A single raft like ours looked like a nutshell on this giant sea-like expanse. The waves crashed over our raft and washed away many of our belongings, anything that was not tied down. We would find ourselves tossed from the top of a wave to the bottom, and when we were at the bottom the high waves towered over us; it seemed we would be swamped at any minute, that the currents would drag us down to our deaths. Once we got stuck on a hidden sandbank and couldn't push off. Again, Zdzichu had to get off and dislodge us.

The Pinega had various feeder rivers and bays, and it wasn't clear which way to go now. The current carried some rafts into one particular bay which, without help, it was impossible to escape. I remember how someone on the far bank waved and shouted to us, telling us to stick to the right hand side so as not to get caught in this bay. You can imagine how afraid we were the whole time we stayed on this river. It seemed that death would inevitably get us one way or another – through hunger, freezing or drowning. After all, right from the start we had been destined for death.

But it's in these moments, when death stares you in the face, that a human being becomes most determined to stay alive – and we eventually reached the port on the Pinega.

Pinega

Pinega is a smallish town and port on the river of the same name, which flows into a bigger river, the Northern Dwina; this itself flows into the White Sea at Archangel. Poles gathered in Pinega, having survived the journey on the raft, and waited for weeks to get on a boat to Archangel. On the riverbank, a crowd gathered in the hope of seeing their family and friends arriving safely on each new raft. When we moored our own raft and looked around, we recognised two children of about five or six years old. They were our Wujek Ignac's children, Basia and Ludek! They were waiting for their father who was due to come back from Archangel – he had been given work on the boat between there and Pinega. Meeting them was a great joy. Basia and Ludek took us straight to their rented home where they lived with a certain Russian woman. Ciocia Julia burst into tears when she saw us, and soon prepared some water for us to wash in, as we were filthy from the smoke and grime of our raft fire. She gave us something to eat and after a short rest we returned to our raft took our things and put them in the waiting room until it was our turn to get on the boat

We also had to visit an office which registered all the new arrivals. More and more Poles kept turning up, and all of them were crowding into this little river port like bees in a hive. Families gathered on the filthy floor of this freezing waiting room, which was packed out with hungry, dirty, scruffy, smelly exiles, who it was difficult to recognise as human beings. There was a small canteen there where you could buy a little food – if you had money. They did at least give us a ration of bread when we registered, so we could regain our strength a little. For almost a month on the raft we had to make do with what we came across, whether it was a luckily caught fish, gathered mushrooms or food begged from locals, who were very sensitive to the suffering of the poor and never sent away a human being empty-handed.

The worst thing about the port was the lice. They were *huge*, and there were countless numbers of them. They crawled on people, on their things and even all over the floor. Lice symbolise dirt and poverty to the highest degree. Our carers knew this well, and to fight this enemy they invented *voshoboiki*, a kind of chemical chamber for killing lice. Before they put people into boats leaving the port, they made you pass through a "*sanitarnaia obstanovka*", a sanitary cleaning process, and issued documents to confirm you had completed it. They made us go through a wash house, and our belongings were put through the *woszobojka* to destroy all the bugs. With the chemicals and high temperatures, they managed to kill all the lice. The Russians were very proud of this, and often repeated this joke: "*U nas tekhnika bol'shaia, a kul'turu na kilogrammy prodaiut"* – We Russians command the latest in technology, and as for culture, we sell it by the kilogram.

They would put everyone into the washhouses together, men, women and children – what a cultured place this was! All of us were just naked in this chamber. There were three rooms: in the first, they threw water onto red hot stones to create steam, and we thwacked ourselves with birch sticks to increase our circulation; in the second there were various smaller troughs of hot and cold water which we used to wash ourselves, with a medicated paste on your hair to ensure the lice were dead. Once you were clean you went into a third room and got dressed, after scrabbling around a big pile of clothes to find your own.

Now we were clean and had our certificate to prove it, but were still waiting to leave. More people were arriving the whole time, and the pressure grew on this port and its waiting room. People lay on the floor one beside the other, making it hard to get through without stepping on someone. It was densely packed, and it smelt of dirt and body odour. There was a constant buzz of noise: children were crying, the ill were moaning, others were shouting and yelling, yet others cried as they were reunited with their families.

It was hell on earth. And here at this hell at Pinega, I met my cousin Stasia, who I hadn't seen since the day we were first deported, 10 February, although I knew they were deported on the very same day. I recognised her only by her skirt, which she embroidered herself when she was a student at agricultural school in Dubica near Brest-Litovsk. My sister had the same skirt, and had finished at the same college just a couple of months before we were sent away.

Stasia, before the war, had been a beautiful girl, blonde with long plaits, and big, blue eyes. Now, after less than two years in the

Soviet Paradise, all that was left of this beautiful girl was a shadow of a human being. She was trying to get through the crowd, among the tatty luggage scattered over the dirty floor, and was gazing around. No doubt she was looking out to see if she could spot someone from the family. I looked and thought I must know this girl, that I recognised her from somewhere, but just couldn't place who or from where. She looked like a zombie, like someone had dug her up from the grave – pale, thin, with sunken, lifeless eyes.

It struck me that she wasn't walking, but seemed to be floating towards us in the air. I may have been hallucinating. She had an open mouth from which she was forcing out the word "Zooosia... Zooosia." It was only when they both fell into each others arms, crying, that I came to my senses and realised that this wasn't a vision or a zombie, but that I really was seeing this girl, a person who was actually alive, and none other than my cousin Stasia. It was a terrible realisation. She didn't have the strength to talk. Scurvy had destroyed her teeth, which were rattling in her gums and, I later saw, came out when pulled. Her front teeth were already missing and she looked like an old lady, even though she was only 21.

After we met with Stasia, the officer read out the names of the families who had to prepare themselves for the next leg of the journey, this time by steamer – our name was among them. This time bread was given out for the journey. Zosia, as the eldest of us, had the honour to go with the documents to get the bread. Unfortunately, not everything that begins well ends well. Zosia went to get the bread, while we boarded the boat. Everything was ready to go, but Zosia still hadn't returned. The captain gave the signal for us to go, but there was still no Zosia. My mother begged the captain to wait just a second, that her daughter had just gone for bread and would be back any moment. No pleading would help though, and the boat slowly started to depart. Then we saw her, running with her suitcase, waving her hands, crying for us to wait. We all cried and begged the captain to stop, because we had only just started to move. But no-one would listen to us – the boat left. Poor, poor Zosia, standing by the side of the river with a suitcase of bread and all our documents. She didn't know where her family were going – or what on earth she was supposed to do. She herself can tell us what happened to her.

CHAPTER 6 – ZOSIA'S STORY

A sanitary cleansing was held to delouse us all, and to disinfect our clothes. About twenty people were put through the bath-house at once, women, men and children together. Our things were thrown into a large oven, a *woszobojka*, to get rid of the lice. On exiting the baths, we had to wait naked in a cold room until our clothes were thrown to us. Then, everyone had to look for their own items and get dressed as quickly as possible. It would often turn out that in their haste, people just put on the first things that came to hand, and so we emerged from this hygienic process in other people's clothes. But it was important that you didn't leave naked.

After this whole operation, we prepared to be loaded onto the boat. We were to be given bread for the road, and so I took all our documents and went to get it. I had to stand for a long time in a queue. Suddenly, I heard the signal that our boat was leaving. I ran with all the strength I had, but the boat was already moving off from the bank. I saw how my mother, brothers and sister were crying, and how my mother was pointing me out to the captain – but with no luck. They floated away, and I, alone as an orphan, was left behind by myself. A black despair overwhelmed me. I didn't know where they were going or where they would be offloaded. I returned to the port, where lots of military men and NKVD had gathered. I was terrified: I was a young, defenceless woman and anyone could easily have harmed me. Then I saw our Polish soldiers, with their commanding officer. I ran to them in tears: "My family's gone, I don't know where, and I don't know what to do," I cried. "Not only that, I was even robbed last night. They turned the light off last night and when I woke this morning my suitcase was stolen, with all our bread in and all our documents. Out in the corridor I spotted the suitcase and I opened it with relief, but they cut a hole out of the back. They left the bread, but took all the money."

I told all this to our Polish soldiers. Their commanding officer had a whip-round among his men for a few roubles to help me on the journey – but I refused to take the money. Instead, their commander suggested I go with them to England, or wherever they were being sent. They were going to join General Anders' army, and really tried hard to talk me into it, but again I refused. I only had one thing in my mind: my family, and how to rejoin them. I asked them just to get me onto the next boat, which was the last transport out of there that winter – it was October and the river was already beginning to freeze up. The captain agreed. They stood around me so the Russians didn't see a civilian boarding, and we made it on without the guards spotting me. Unfortunately, this good luck was short-lived: they made an inspection and threw off all the civilians on the boat. They were shouting *"vylezai na bereg! Nel'zia! A to na silu vybrosim!"* – Get out onto the bank, it's prohibited for you to be here! Or we'll throw you out!

What was there to do? I'd made it 40km of the way, and yet again I found myself abandoned at a tiny little river port – but now on the giant River Dwina. I stood here and had no idea what to do. I was scared to pieces and utterly lost. But all of a sudden, I see a boat coming from Archangel, and it's slowly coming towards my port because they'd seen people standing there – every so often, it seems, they had come across people like me, thrown off military boats. It was increasingly cold, and the river was freezing over, so the boat had to move very slowly. That's when I heard: "Zosia! Zosia!" I couldn't believe my ears.

I thought I was hearing things because of my exhaustion and fear. However, I left my little group and walked right up to the shore, only to see... Wujek Ignac, crying out and waving his hands! I shouted back, "Wujek! Wujek!", and cried with relief. The boat moored and my uncle took me straight to his cabin, where he fed me and said, "Don't worry about the family. They are at Camp Warda: your mum with the children and Wujek Janek with his family."

He took me back to Pinega, and tried to work out how I could get there and join them. Pinega to Warda was a long way, about 60km. How was I to get there? Wujek wasn't going in that direction, only to Archangel. He advised me that I could stick to the bank of the Pinega and just walk until I got to Warda. So I left early the next morning with my suitcase. I had all the documents and the bread, so I could eat on the way. I walked quickly during the day, because I had to find places to sleep at night. At times I even ran so as to cover as much ground as possible before night. For long periods there was nowhere to stay, and I worried that the wolves would eat me at night.

Eventually I saw some kind of barracks by the side of the river, which were sometimes used for loggers. I was pleased that if I didn't find a village I could at least stay here. It was getting darker, but still I ran further in the hope that I'd find a settlement, because I was afraid I might freeze to death in the barracks. Being alone in such an isolated place, surrounded by wolves, also filled me with fear. I ran and I cried and I prayed, until eventually I found a collective farm. I ran to the first house I saw and knocked on the door.

The woman who opened the door was very surprised to see a young girl alone so late at night. She let me in and listened to my story. With her husband she looked over my documents, and they explained that to stay the night on the *kolkhoz* you were supposed to report in earlier – but they didn't send me away. The woman told me to call her Ciocia Irena. She was very sympathetic, and her husband was a very good man too. They sat me at the table with them, fed me, poured me hot *kipiatok* from their samovar, and put me to sleep on the stove, where I was warm and safe. The next morning after breakfast I asked them how far it was to Warda; they said it would take me a whole week to get there! In the end, it took me five days.

At Warda I was recognised by an acquaintance, who told me that my family lived in Barrack 10, and had been enormously worried about me. From the river stop you had to climb a giant staircase up a hill to the barracks. Luckily, as I was walking up those stairs I met my cousin Krysia, the oldest daughter of Wujek Janek. Krysia was going with a can to the canteen to collect some soup. I waited for her, and we went together to the family barracks. At my appearance, crying and happiness were mixed together. There was a general celebration that we were all together again.

I looked like *półtora nieszczęścia*, as we say – "150% misery". My legs were running with wounds, and swollen to a giant size, and the blood that had dripped down my legs had dried between my toes. My mother boiled some water with pine tree buds, and soaked my legs in this water – that brought me some relief. I discovered that in the time I'd been away, more than a week, they wouldn't give my family any bread, because they didn't have their documents. I still had some bread in my suitcase, so we finally ate it together. The next day, even though my legs were in bandages and still in great pain, I went to the office, showed them our papers, and received ration cards. I wanted them to give us the bread in arrears which they'd kept from my family for a week. They told me, *molchi!* – shut up!

Zosia (left), with Zdzichu and our cousin Stasia, Hipolit Król's daughter.

The director of this camp was an extremely unpleasant man. He didn't have a right hand, and wrote with his left. He was incredibly sadistic, and hated the Poles. He called us *pany, burżuje, bieloruczki* – gentlemen, rich landowners, light-skinned aristocrats and so forth. They warned me about him, but in anger that he had starved my family, I told him that God had punished him for his unpleasantness by taking away his hand. He cursed at me in Russian in such disgusting language I'm ashamed to repeat it. Again he told me to shut up, if I valued my life. Then he asked me when I was going to get work – because he who doesn't work, doesn't eat.

The next day I went to see a doctor. She was a good, normal person, and gave me a week's sick leave, and after that, another week. So only after two weeks was I set back to work.

CHAPTER 7 – WORK CAMP WARDA: A NEW HELL

At the end of August or beginning of September 1942, our boat unloaded us at the Warda labour camp, which was located on the Northern Dwina, about 100km from Archangel. The Northern Dwina flows into the White Sea, which joins the Arctic Ocean near the Arctic Circle. On one side of this enormous northern river lay the Taiga, and on the other were collective farms and Chołmogory, a small town about which the Russian writer Vera Panova wrote in her 1955 novel, *Seryozha*. Unfortunately, we were placed in another forest labour camp, not a collective farm like the *kolkhozy*. Again, we faced forestry work, and again extreme hunger.

Warda, at least the side where we lived, was alongside the river, which was reached by a giant staircase from the top of the hill. This was almost impossible to climb in winter, when the stairs were frozen over, and you had to slide down on your bottom. Immediately on our arrival we were placed in our lodgings, which was something like the wagon in which we were deported from Poland. On one side was a double bench, on the other side another, but between them was a corridor so narrow two people couldn't pass. One side was put aside for the five of us, and and the other for my uncle's family, so there were ten people cramped in a tiny space. You couldn't get dressed or undressed standing up. You either had to go out in the corridor, or get dressed lying down on the wooden beds. They told us that we would only be here temporarily, until they found us better living quarters. In this barracks lived political prisoners from Latvia and Lithuania, all men, sent to the gulags for hard labour for their political activities. They called them enemies of the Soviet Union.

A severe winter descended with great speed. Most of the day passed in darkness, with just two or three hours a day of sunlight. It snowed almost constantly outside, and our barrack was extremely cold. There was only a small stove connected to the tiny corridor; Tadek was still too young to work, but he was in charge of chopping wood to keep us warm. We were extremely hungry too, because there was nowhere to cook. As before, our bread ration was 800g for workers; but "*izhdiventsy*" – children, old people and anyone else who didn't work – received only 200g per day. When they were in season, my brother Tadzio and I would pick mushrooms and berries, and trade them for a little extra bread. Fortunately, we did not stay very long in these barracks, and it was still winter when they moved us to a bigger room with a cooker, so we could prepare our own food. Apart from us and my uncle's family, more people lived in this new room – but at least it was fairly warm. The food situation was worse; there wasn't enough bread. You could buy soup, pasta or kasza in the canteen but there wasn't enough money for that kind of luxury. We had to settle in for a nine-month winter, trying to find some food at any cost.

Women with children went across the river to the collective farms to try to feed their families. They bartered possessions for food – dresses, rings, watches, anything they still had left. We ate everything it was possible to get. In desperation, my Ciocia Andzia cooked a fantastic kind of jelly from a soldier's belt! First she soaked this pigskin strap for a long time, then boiled it for ages. When it was soft, she sliced it very thin and let the brown boiling water, now full of gelatine, set around it. The end product was very bitter – but edible.

I remember once when someone said that "today we will have a dinner party." We were all very excited about this. Eventually, the men turned up with a lot of fresh meat. The washing and frying soon began. To this day I remember the smell, which filled the room and tantalised our nostrils. Our saliva was running as if we were hungry animals! We couldn't wait for this promised feast. At last, on our pine-tree table, two dishes of fried, aromatic meat were set, and we were invited to dine. We threw ourselves on this food like hungry wolves, chewing and licking each bone to the last. It was the first time in two years we had had meat – and to satisfaction! It was only after we had eaten it all that we discovered we had been eating *dog*, which the men had bought in exchange for vodka. Well then – you have to eat something.

There were many animals in the Taiga, but we had no weapons to kill them with, and it was an imprisonable offence to set traps. One of the Poles came up with a song:

> *My na Wardzie żiwiom, charaszo pitajemsia,*
> *Wsiu koninu piereieli, na sabak brasajemsia!*
> (We live in Warda, we eat very well. We've eaten all the dead horses, and we're now throwing ourselves on the dogs.)

They sang this in Russian – it was called a *czastushka* and was a kind of folk verse, usually humorous – and danced around. After her recovery, Zosia was somewhat cheered up, thanks to the good doctor, and was recommended to work in a *sovkhoz* called Bashary, in a greenhouse, a story which she will tell herself.

Baszary farm – Zosia's account

"Thanks to the doctor who gave me the permit to say I couldn't work in the forest, I was instead directed to a farm. The work was in the gardens and in fields. We built lots of greenhouses for various kinds of vegetables. The climate was very severe and things would only grow in the greenhouses. The work was hard because we had to build all these structures ourselves. You had to pierce the frozen land with a metal pickaxe, throw it to one side, and pour in compost in its place, mixed with a natural manure and sand. Only then could we put seeds in.

"The farm was big, about 50ha. There were cows, pigs and a beautiful horse called Karina, who I used to ride. The director was a handsome and good man, educated in military college. He inspected all the works on his horse. Many Poles worked there. He treated us very humanely and talked with us a good deal. There was a kitchen there, and the food was reasonable. Two months after building the greenhouse, our plantings sprang up – salad, radishes, cucumbers and potatoes. Unfortunately, these luxuries weren't for exiles like us, only for the people in charge.

"Despite this, and the fact they kept a watch over us, from time to time we managed to eat some of these vitamins – so conditions were very different to when we were in the forest. However, we could not remove anything on pain of imprisonment. Once I covered for a woman who was looking after the cattle, feeding, watering and milking the cows. Then I had a great time, because I could drink all the milk I wanted. Once I found a bottle and tied it in my trouser leg, and in this manner I carried out this milk to my sister Ala, who was ill. Only good nutrition could save her life, according to the doctor. Sadly, this work soon finished, and the hardship began again."

Our "new house": the adventure in the Taiga

Spring came, and with spring we moved to a new house which, as I recall, was newly built and two storeys high, with three one-bedroomed accommodations downstairs, and three upstairs, one bedroom allocated per family. We lived upstairs. Under us lived the Szostek family, our neighbours from Suszki. On each floor there was a corridor and a toilet. There must, therefore, have been some form of running water and pipework, but I don't remember this specifically.

In each room was a big wooden-bench bed, a table and bench, and a stove so we could cook. The worst thing was the sleeping, five of us on one bed. So we slept *na waleta* – like the kings and queens on playing cards, head to foot. Mum, Zosia and I had our heads on one side of the bed, and Zdzichu and Tadek had the other side, with our legs mixed between us. We covered ourselves with a quilt and whatever else was possible, in order to be warm. It was a very tight fit in there.

There was no wardrobe for our things. We had a trunk we'd brought from Poland, and we kept our belongings in there. This trunk is an important souvenir for us, because it lasted six years of exile, and returned back to Poland together with us. Now it's in Sitno, in the home we moved into when we returned from Russia, where my mother lived until her death in May 1995.

This accommodation at Warda was one of the best that we'd had up till now – small but at least private. Next to us, across the corridor, lived a family with many children. With their daughter Regina, who was somewhere between Tadek and me in age, we would go to the forest to gather mushrooms and pick berries. Once the three of us went with Zosia to gather mushrooms and we got lost. This was a terribly frightening experience. At first when we went into the forest all was fine; the forest hummed safely, we were warm and felt secure. The red hats of *krashnuk* mushrooms, kings of the forest, popped up here and there, and it was pleasant to run around the forest picking them.

When our baskets were full of mushrooms, we realised that we no longer knew where we were. We sought some forest paths, and ran around shouting, barefoot and frightened to death, until it began to get dark and to drizzle. Suddenly, someone replied to our calls with a cry of their own. Calling to each other, we met with a group of Russian women by the lake, one which we'd never heard about before. We learned from them that on this lake there was a big saw-mill camp, where they were heading. We, on the other hand, wanted to get to our camp Warda, which was situated on the bank of the Dwina.

No-one knew what direction to go in to get to their destination. After a short consultation they decided to go to the right. Zosia said, "Since they are going to the right to get to the saw-mill, we should go to the left to get to the river." Fortunately my sister guessed right. It was getting ever darker and we were scared, but Zosia was singing and picking mushrooms, saying things like "What a lovely mushroom, we can't leave this one!" No doubt she was also scared but she wanted to keep it from us, to stop us getting too frightened. She was the eldest, and responsible for our security. Poor Zosia had to worry inside herself because she knew what could happen if we didn't get out of this forest. We didn't have any matches, so couldn't make a fire, and without this we wouldn't stand a chance of surviving till morning.

Luck was on our side. The path before us began to clear, but it still wasn't obvious to us whether we were approaching the river or the unknown lake. It was already almost dark, but the path was well-trodden so we continued walking. Surely, people walked to the saw-mill along this path? This was our salvation. We walked on a little more and found ourselves on our riverbank. What a reprieve! We hugged each other and wept with relief. We didn't know how far we were from home but we knew that we would get their eventually, that the river would lead us there.

Before us along the river burnt a fire, where a few people sat, but we were scared to approach these strangers. We circled them through the forest and returned to the river, and carried on walking along the riverbank. Our sister cheered us up by telling us she knew where we were and that we would soon be at home. In the meantime, mum, Zdzichu and Regina's family had really begun to worry and had let the commandant know that we had gone mushroom picking and still hadn't returned. The commandant organised some people to begin searching for us. In such cases they would bang a gong and shine torches as part of their search party, shouting "Hup, hup!" We heard this cry, and replied with the same, and soon saw before us our brother and two Russians who had come out to find us. Our mother waited at home, the tears streaming down her face. We were frozen and wet to the bone. That night I got a high temperature and developed pneumonia, which would lead to many problems with my health,
which I describe later.

Winter came again, and again hunger and deprivation attacked our community. People suffered and were dying en masse. My friend Regina died of tuberculosis. Another friend, Władzia Szostek, who I'd gone to primary school with back home in Suszki, died of the scurvy and swelling brought on by starvation.

The Szostek family lived below us so I visited Władzia often. Her mother also died of the same maladies that killed Władzia. Both suffered greatly. They were swollen all over, and their thighs had open sores that gaped right down to the bone. People whispered that Władzia's father ate their rations of bread, saying that their 200g ration would not save them anyway now, that they would die regardless and that by not eating it, they would shorten their suffering – and at least their rations might save his life. Maybe he was right.

I feared death greatly. I didn't want to die. I was still so young, just 14. There was a beautiful pine tree nearby, where I used to go and pray, thinking that this tall tree might go all the way up to God: I begged for a miracle, that I wouldn't die in this frozen land. At the very least I prayed for a single potato to eat before I died. I didn't go to school because I was constantly ill – not just with pneumonia, but with pleurisy and tuberculosis of the glands. I looked like a skeleton and had it not been for the bravery of my mother I would no doubt have gone to the same place as my friends, and hundreds of other exiled prisoners. My mother, since becoming a widow at a young age, had learned how to fight for the existence of her young children. She was intelligent and very brave; she knew how to win people's trust; she was able to write in Russian as well as speak it; and she was an excellent dress-maker.

Here, in exile, she had to work in the forests, where her own health sufferred, to the extent that the camp's medical board recognised her as a second-degree invalid. She remained exempt from heavy-duty labour in the forest. During the time she didn't work, she managed to cross the river to the *kolkhozy* to exchange goods for food. She made friends with the Siberian women, for whom she made new clothes from old items, for which they paid with food.

Once she brought us a kilogram of butter, which she got from the wife of the chairman of the collective farm – but only in exchange for her gold wedding ring. Sometimes she brought potatoes, some flour, some Russian pasties, whatever it was possible to get. There was always great happiness when mum came back after a few days' absence with bags of food. I'm certain that her actions saved our lives.

My doctor Marusia wept as she told me that I wouldn't die as long as I had *rybii zhir i khoroshee pitanie* – cod liver oil and nourishing food. Cod liver oil wasn't an easy prospect. Tou couldn't get it, even on prescription – there simply wasn't any. There wasn't *any* kind of medicine there. If you had a cold, they prescribed *banoczki*, glass balls, heated then stuck on the skin to "draw out" the illness. For pleurisy they made compresses from mustard seeds. For chicken-blindness they prescribed a few grams of liver from a dead horse. For scurvy they told you to eat bark from birch trees and raw potatoes, or dry vegetables which you couldn't find in this region even if you had a candle. I was told to expose my chest to sunshine to dry out the water.

Cod liver oil was the best medicine for all illnesses, but to get a bottle of it, you had to get yourself to Archangel, 100km from Warda, where there was a Polish consulate which received aid from the US and England for Polish people in exile. My mother was a member of the Union of Polish Patriots, and she discovered at their meetings that you could get help at Archangel, so she decided to go to this miracle city, in the middle of winter, with her sister-in-law. The two women went off, pulling little sledges behind them, so that they could bring the promised treasures back on them. It was an awful winter, thick with snow and ice. Snowstorms and snowdrifts cut at their legs, but they walked, their heads covered in scarves and shawls, their legs in felt boots, dressed up in felt jackets and trousers, covered with snow. They pushed themselves on – and on, and on.

On foot to Archangel

My mother and aunt stopped in the *kolkhoz* overnight, where they were welcomed and offered hot food, *kipiatok* from the samovar, whatever they had to share. They laid themselves to sleep on big Russian stoves to keep warm. In the morning they were also given breakfast, after which they set off on their long journey. They often had to move off the road to give way to a big lorry or tractor. Then they would fall into deep snow, from which it was almost impossible to climb out. Occasionally a kind *kolkhoznik* (farmer) would stop and tell them to get onto his sledge, and would take them along a while before he turned off the road. The inhabitants of the far north were good people. They didn't have much themselves, but they shared everything that they had with others who needed it. They had large, gentle hearts, and understood the meaning of hunger, cold and slavery.

At last the travellers stopped in a village near Archangel. In this village there was a *kirpicznyj zawod* – a brick-making factory where many Poles worked. Talking with the Poles, they discovered that my Wujek Marcel now worked there, husband of our Ciocia Hela – mum's sister – and that he lived here with his whole family. How to describe the joy when these two sisters and their sister-in-law met again? Up until this moment they had known nothing about each others' fates. The last time they had seen each other was in the cattle wagons being transported into the unknown.

It turns out that when they had transported us all in 1940, my uncle slipped and broke his leg. He was taken to hospital in Archangel, and Hela categorically refused to go further without her husband. She had four small children: the oldest daughter, Urszula, was only 13, Rysiu was 11 and Ludek 10, and the youngest daughter, Kamila, was about 6. Ciocia Hela wept desperately, and cried that without her husband she couldn't take her children anywhere. The commandant's heart softened at these words, and he let them stay. Through the misfortune of my uncle, the family benefited in the long run. They had settled near Archangel on the main artery of the Northern Dwina – in other words, protected from the deepest Taiga. Being on the river meant they could sail to the large sea ports, windows to the world, and the centre of northern culture and civilization. In Archangel there was a kind of Polish consulate called a *delegatura* which provided information and limited help for Poles. There were only two Polish embassies in the whole USSR, in Moscow and Kuibishev, but these *delegatury* could be found in some of the smaller cities.

Yes, my uncle's family were in a good place indeed, because when General Anders was recruiting to his army, my uncle was able to join them with his family, and in 1942 they marched away from Soviet slavery. We tried to join the army too, but were told that we would depart in a second mass transportation. As it turned out, this was only arranged in 1946, so we had four more painful years to wait.

My mother's return; my brother's arrest; Archangel
When my mother returned from Archangel, she brought back many desperately needed articles: not only cod liver oil, but flour and bread, frozen on the sledge (she'd travelled 100km to get two loaves of bread); some fat, powdered eggs, preserved meat and a few pieces of clothing. You can imagine our joy at mum's return, and at all the items she'd

brought with her. After her journey the consulate sent aid to our camp several times, since they now knew that Poles were out here. The people who most benefited from these parcels were those who worked in the consulate distributing parcels, of course. It's often like that in life, and we have a saying about it: *Bliższa ciału koszula niż sukienka* – the underwear is closer to the body than the dress.

Spring arrived. In the meantime I had been very ill with water in my left lung, and had been hospitalised for treatment. The hospital was in Archangel, 100km from the camp, and the only way to get there was by river – but the river was full of melting ice. Icebergs from the river, which formed around frozen logs, were piling up like Egyptian pyramids. These pyramids had to be blown up with dynamite, and the logs caught with metal hooks so they could be brought individually onto the bank of the river. This was the only way to stop the ice piling up, because there was a danger they they would flood the area when they melted. This logging work was a very dangerous operation, and experts in the field had to sort the problem out.

My doctor Marusia was very worried about me. She saved me with glass *banki* and mustard seed compresses – she could do nothing else. Hunger was threatening to kill us, because my mother could no longer cross the river to the collective farm, and no mushrooms or berries were growing in the forests. You could find a few cranberries on overgrown lakes (more like bogs, really), because they lasted over winter under the snow, and there was also a special raspberry we called *morożka*, which grew in marshy ground, on very low bushes. It was very sweet, a yellow-orangey colour, big and juicy. People would go out exploring for these berries – as would we, with our mum – because they were rich in vitamin C, particularly the cranberries. But it was very dangerous to pick them, because you had to know how to jump from one solid place to another, and where the boggy parts were. People would fall up to their waists in the water and it was difficult to get them out. We were forbidden to go there at dusk for it was certain death. Indeed, many people drowned in these marshes.

My sister often saved some bread from her ration and brought it to us from the forest. Through her kindness she herself weakened, and would sometimes collapse. Zosia and Zdzichu worked hard, but earned so little they could only buy our ration of bread for the family. People did what they could to get food and stole whenever they had a chance. But if somebody was caught stealing, they were severely punished.

You were not allowed to take anything, even rotten potatoes which were lying in the fields in spring. Guards rode round on horses and whipped people stealing from fields. Once Ciocia Andzia came home with a lash across her face after such an expedition to the *kolkhoz*. Our "carers" said, *"Chto kazennoe nie tron', a tronesh', to tiur'ma"* – "Keep your hands off anything that belongs to the state. Even let it rot, but don't touch it. If you do you will go to prison." And so it was.

But how could you not touch such food when hunger is wiping out your family, and all these creatures around you who once were people, wiping them out from the camps of the nearly living and dispatching them to the forests of eternal rest? Each person there wanted to save the lives of their loved ones – at any cost, even if it meant losing their own lives. I remember how one father of many children, going to the ports for supplies, stoically announced that either he would return with food or he wouldn't return at all. He did not return the way he had wished, but a few days later the river spat him out onto the bank. I saw his awful, swollen corpse. People said that he had been decapitated, but we children were chased away before we saw too much. He had probably fallen into the wheels of a river steam ship, a *kater*.

Several of these boats went down the Dwina from Archangel to Kotlas and back, sometimes stopping at our harbour to deliver goods like flour for baking and other kitchen products. They unloaded their cargo on the bank of the river, but the loads weren't always taken to the store-rooms straight away, and were sometimes left on the banks overnight. A man was left to guard it, but sometimes the younger and more daring Poles would manage to steal something for their families.

My uncle once set out on such an expedition with two others, which ended with him serving two years in prison. They were arrested and sentenced by the court to two years' hard labour in the most severe gulag near Archangel – for stealing one sack of flour. My brother Zdzichu also got two years, for taking two kilos of potatoes. He was actually going to collect our rations of bread with a little white pillow case to carry it in. He was passing a winter potato store, an open heap, and one of the local women selecting the potatoes threw some into his pillowcase. Unfortunately a woman on guard duty saw this happen, and immediately dragged him to her office. She didn't listen to any explanation for how these potatoes got into his bag. He tried to convince her that he was on his way to get bread, and if he was going to steal potatoes he would have taken a sack, not a small pillowcase! But no explanation would do him any good. She called for the militia, and they carried him off to the prison in Chołmogory (our district), where he sat until his trial and sentence.

Zdzichu shared a cell with real criminals, thieves and tramps who had sat in prison many a time, and who preferred to be there than free, because at least they fed them in prison. These were scary, dirty men with long, tangled beards, as my mother later described them. My brother was still a child, about 19, and cried like a child when mum came to visit him. Once she brought him a bottle of milk and told him to drink it in front of her, but the guard took it from his mouth and gave it back to mum, saying, "*Nielzia*" – you can't do that. My mum's heart burst with sadness that such a cruel man wouldn't let her child have a drop of milk. If she brought food to him it was taken to the cell; but the hungry tramps threw themselves on Zdzichu, stole the food, and ate it all themselves.

After the trial they sent him to the same gulag that they'd sent my mother's brother to. There he had a bit of luck. He was young and handsome, and the doctor took a shine to him, so she saved him by writing a certificate of exemption from hard work. Thanks to the doctor, my brother was put on a special nourishing diet which she prescribed as his medication. And what's more, he had a pass beyond the prison boundaries to the free zone; here he would meet really good people who fed him, and he could even bring something back for his uncle to alleviate his starvation.

In 1944, thanks to the 1941 amnesty and various other international treaties, they transported many of us from the north to Ukraine. At this point all the non-serious prisoners were released, even though their sentences had not been completed. At this time my Ciocia Andzia, me and Balbina, the youngest daughter of my uncle, travelled to bring our imprisoned relatives back. We stood in front of the huge gate and waited for them. Balbina saw her father first and shouted, "*tatuś, tatuś*". Having heard this, the guard shouted, "*Nielza!*" and chased us away from the gate. Despite this, our reunion was very emotional, with tears flowing between the hugs and kisses.

We sailed together back to our camp. My brother never forgot, until the end of his life, that I came to get him from the gulag prison. He was always grateful, and always helped me when I needed it.

Zosia, Zdzichu and Tadzio some years after we returned to Poland. They were 26, 23 and 16 respectively when we left Siberia.

CHAPTER 8 – IN ARCHANGEL

Soon after our brother was released, we noticed that boats began to travel the route to Archangel more frequently. This was fortunate for me, since I was diagnosed with pleurisy, and had been referred to the hospital in Archangel for an operation. My mother and I went together, taking an address for our friends, the Gołębiowski family, from back in Suszki, with whom we had lived in Kołos. We stayed with them overnight. One of Mrs Gołębiowski's sons worked in a flourmill and brought home scraped-together leavings of dirty flour, which they used to bake bread cakes.

Mrs Gołębiowski fed us with some *placki* (pancakes) for dinner, and again for breakfast the next day. After breakfast mum and I set off to the hospital. The doctor was very kind, and after examining me told us to return tomorrow, and in the meantime he would find me a bed in the hospital. So the next day my mum and I went to the tram stop in the morning, walking on a kind of wooden pavement. All the wooden boards were loose and moved around, and you had to be careful not to have an accident. If you stood on one end of a board, the other end could flip up and hit you in the head!

When we got to the city centre there were real pavements for walking. The hospital was located on one main road, which was called Paulina Winogradowa street, a streetname I remember very well. Mum and I were standing at the tram stop and waiting when, suddenly, mum collapsed! She lay on the pavement with her eyes rolling up into her head. I began yelling for help. Some people arrived and put her into a seat on the tram, opening the windows as the tram moved on. I stood

next to mum, talking to her, shaking her, caressing her – but she gave
no reply.

   She wouldn't react to anything, and for all the world it looked
like she was dead. When we reached the hospital, two men took my
mother under the arms and carried her to my doctor. He immediately
turned his attention to her: it transpired that she had developed typhus,
or bloody dysentery as we also called it. An ambulance immediately
took my mother to a closed hospital for contagious diseases. They took
me too, but I could only look at mum though a window. I stood, I
watched, and I cried. Frightened and alone, I returned to our family
friends, unsure of what was going to happen to my mother.

   The next day I returned. The doctor told me that my mother
was extremely ill and would have to remain in hospital for two weeks.
She was being given a series of injections, and had been placed on a
strict diet – but everything should be fine. I managed to speak to my
mother through the window; she told me that she felt better already and
advised me to go to my doctor. I did something entirely different, as I
was hungry and had a little money that I had made by selling berries in
the queue at the dock. I walked along streets, and saw ham and sausage
on display in shop windows. This was just what I fancied, so I went into
the shop and asked for a little sausage, but the cashier told me that what
I had seen in the window was just an advert – that it was painted on
wood and that it was not real! You could only get certain items like
sausage with special ration cards. So I went further on. Eventually,
I found myself in a marketplace selling various foods, even bread.
After putting aside some money for travel, I bought some bread, and
kept a little aside for a portion of soup. Eating my bread, I carried on
in search of a canteen.

All of a sudden I heard music, and a procession emerged along the street, complete with an orchestra. I saw sailors, but they didn't look like Soviet sailors, and although they were carrying a coffin covered with a flag, it was not the Russian flag. These mariners were tall and handsome – somehow different from Russians. Many people stood watching the procession, and I asked one man who these sailors were. He told me that these were English navy men, that they had a military base in Archangel, and that what I was watching was a funeral of an English sailor. He was going to be buried at sea, as was traditional. To this day I do not know whether this was true or not, although I later discovered that Murmansk and Archangel housed both English and Polish military bases.

I was completely enchanted with this sight, and in the excitement I lost my purse with all my money. This could have been a complete disaster, but luckily it was picked up by an honest man who shouted behind me, "*Devushka, vy uronili koshelek*" – girl, you've dropped your purse – and handed it over. Oh my God! What would I have done without money? I was only 14, terrified and lost in this busy port city. Even with my purse back I did not know what to do, since I couldn't stay here much longer and had so little money, just enough for a ticket. So I decided to return all the way home to Warda. And so, instead of mum leaving me in hospital, I left mum there.

When I returned Zosia and Tadek were naturally very worried about our mother's typhus, because it was incredibly rare to survive this illness. But my doctor had assured me that she would recover, and so it came to pass. In two weeks she returned home and we were together again. As a family we decided to move across the river to where the *kolkhozy* were, to Chołmogory.

CHAPTER 9 – OUR LAST STOP IN THE FAR
NORTH OF RUSSIA – CHOŁMOGORY

Chołmogory was an important district town in the Archangel region – a region that was itself bigger than Poland. Important regional government offices were based there, as well as a court, a hospital, railway and a major river port. There must have been many kinds of shops and restaurants or canteens, but I don't remember, because I was only there three times – once in the hospital, once in the court and once in the prison.

We lived in a *sovkhoz*, a state farm, right near the town. Many Poles lived there. There was work in the fields, but none in the forest, as we had been doing up to now. As such, we had a better chance of survival. I remember very well how we crossed the Dwina on a rowing boat because there was no bridge. The waves were huge, and tossed the boat around like a nutshell, first down – and it seemed to me like we were going to the bottom of the river – then to the very top of the wave, and it felt like we were thrown into the air. I was incredibly scared that these huge waves would carry us with them, but the rowers were very skilful and experienced, and cut into the waves with the boat's prow: had the boat been caught side-on it would have been the end of us.

My imagination worked into such a fever of terror that I actually lost my memory and all I can remember is that the next day I was in the hospital, as I had fallen unconscious as a result of the fear and my illness. Later, mum told me that when we arrived at the *sovkhoz* I'd developed such a high temperature that I had been rushed to hospital immediately. Now I can remember how I lay on the wooden trolley in the corridor because there was no place for a bed in the ward.

When one old lady died I was invited to lie on her bed, but I cried terribly, afraid that I would die straight away if I got in. I did not want to be the next one to go.

Another ill lady saved me from this situation by offering me her bed. It turned out that I'd contracted malaria, which could only be cured with bitter yellow tablets of quinine. At first I had a terrible fever, and my temperature could only be kept down with iced compresses. The food in hospital was very good and genuinely sufficient and filling. Throughout the four years of our exile in the north I had never had food as satisfying as in this hospital.

After my recovery, I returned to my family in the *sovkhoz*. Here once again we had to fight hunger to survive. This *sovkhoz* had been a monastery in the time of the Czars, and was a very interesting place. There was a Russian Orthodox church and some of the older dormitories were beautiful, with original towers and domes. There was an office there, central administration for the *sovkhozy*, and different farm buildings surrounded it. Behind the monastery lay a lake, and it was said that the Communists had murdered all the monks and drowned their bodies in the lake. The natives told us in great secrecy that the waters of the lake had long been red with the blood of the murdered, and that there had been an outbreak of rats who had gorged themselves on the dead bodies.

We were housed in barracks, but within this we had a large private room, in which was two wooden benches, a stove to heat the room, and an iron stove for cooking. Our friends the Logwinowicz family had settled there before us, and lived in one of the former monastery buildings. Its walls were thick as fortress walls, and beneath it were large cellars. Either side of the corridors down here were rows of cells, and the walls still bore smears of blood from the murder of the monks. The Russian women often claimed that there were ghosts in this monastery, and Mrs Logwinowicz said that, after dark, she could hear moans and screaming rising up from under the floor. All this naturally scared us children, but it was also quite exciting, and didn't stop us from night-time visits to the barn, when Mrs Lewandowska stayed up with the birthing cows to ensure the calves were safely delivered.

The worst bit was finding our way to the barn at night, without being caught by the guards; this would have been the end of us and Mrs Lewandowska. Fortunately, we always managed it, and once there things were fine. My friend Lonia's mother took a little milk from one cow and a little from another, and we drank as much of this as we could. Sometimes Mrs Lewandowska baked *placki* for us with oats meant for the cow, and they tasted wonderful with the fresh milk.

Unfortunately, we couldn't take anything home for our families for obvious reasons, so we took turns going out there. One time I would go with Lonia, another time Tadek would go with her sister Teresa – and only when the night was very dark. Fear pressed down on our shoulders as we crept, partly because we were scared of ghosts, partly because we were scared to be caught. But hunger was the strongest fear of all, and dispelled the others.

The church at the *sovkhoz* had been converted into a store room. Various machines had been lined up along one side, and on the other side they had built a large wooden container for grain. My mother worked there airing the grain, stirring it around with a wide shovel to prevent it turning mouldy. Sometimes she managed to sneak

My friend Teresa Lewandowska with her grandmother in 1930,
aged three or four. She brought this picture from Poland and gave
it to me in Chołmogory in 1944.

home some rye or barley grain, concealed in her trouser legs or shoes. We ground these grains down into flour, and used them as the basis for a kind of soup called *muczanka*. Her position in the granary thus saved us – but only for a short while, because things changed when she fell ill. Our mother was in hospital, my brother far away in an Archangel gulag, and by bad luck Zosia's shoes had been sent to the cobblers for repairs, so she couldn't go to work for a few days. For this, she was branded a *progulsczic*, someone who absconded from work and was unable to produce a doctor's certificate.

To punish her "offence", they stopped our family's bread rations – not only Zosia's, but all of them. We found ourselves in a tragic position, starved and degraded, reduced to begging around the Russian villages, calling on their charity in the name of Christ. Once when I was out begging with my friend Władzia, a flash of black soil on the road side caught our eyes. We discovered an empty pit used for storing turnips for animal feed. Our minds were swimming with hunger and desperation, and we began to dig around in the hope of finding a leftover turnip.

While we crawled in the muck on our hands and knees, we heard somebody calling, and saw a woman running towards us, shouting, "Girls, girls, wait for me." So we waited: we didn't come to steal, so we weren't scared. We had simply stopped on the way to the village, carrying only small bags with us for donations.

Chołmogory; an arrest; and the barrister
The woman ran up to us short of breath and, taking us firmly under her arms, asked quite sweetly, "Girls, will you take me to the *sovkhoz*?" But we soon realised that there was something wrong. We told this woman

that we were on our way to the village, but she held us tightly, insisting that we take her to the *sovkhoz* – because, she claimed, she was not local. We had no choice but to go with her; if we had not, she could have dragged us there by force. She was a big, strong woman, and we were two little starvelings.

So we pretended that we didn't suspect her trick, and went along with her. When we arrived at the office, she reported that she had caught some thieves, and demanded the militia. In the meantime, Zosia happened to come to the same office. Seeing me there, she took me by the arm and said, "And what are you doing here? Let's go home." But this woman, clearly an NKVD loyalist, didn't let her, repeating her accusation and explaining that she had caught us in a state store-pit, stealing turnips. "*Szto kazionnoie nie troń, a troniesz, to tiurma*," she announced – that which belongs to the state, must not be touched, or its prison for you. You may let it rot, but don't dare touch it.

After a while two militia men arrived, their rifles slung over their shoulders, and enquired about the "thieves". When she pointed to us, their faces betrayed their surprise but the next words we heard were still "Let's go." By this time a crowd of bystanders had gathered to see this grimly amusing sight, two tiny starving girls led away under the armed escort of two stony faced militiamen. Their captives, these menaces to the state, were locked in a cell, and told to wait for the commandant. I was scared, remembering with horror how my brother had been sentenced to two years for his two kilograms of potatoes. We had taken nothing, but that did not matter: we had transgressed into a state store-pit, and that could be enough to condemn us.

Night fell, compounding our fears, and still we were waiting for
the commandant. The windows and doors had iron bars on them. We
shook with fear, and could not stop crying. In the meantime, Zosia and
Pola, Władzia's sister, were trying to find us, having started their search
at the prison, because they thought we had been locked up with real
criminals. At last the commandant arrived and he chose me for
questioning. Although I was already 15, I looked about 10. Perhaps
he thought that such a young child would tell the truth, but the older one
may lie. Of course, in this case there was nothing to lie about.

One by one I answered his questions. He could see that I was
telling the truth, and it was obvious to me that he felt sorry for us,
because he murmured under his breath, *"durnaia baba, durnaia baba"*
– what a stupid woman! The investigation soon ended and he set us
free. Zosia and Pola were already waiting for us outside, and we threw
ourselves into their arms. We returned home, where Tadek waited for
us; he was very sad because he had cooked *muczanka*, but much of it
had boiled over and been lost. We shared what was left, and went to
bed in the hope that our bread ration would be returned the next day.

In the morning I went to the *sovkhoz* chairman to get the bread
ration cards, but he recited his doctine: *kto nie rabotaye…* It was too
much for me, and emboldened me to look him in the face and say,
"Well take us back to Poland, then! Why did you bring us here, since
you have nothing to eat yourselves?" He seemed bemused, and retorted
cruelly, *"Ne uvidish' Pol'shu kak sinevo moria"* – you will never see
Poland again, just as you will never see the blue sea. Needless to say,
he did not give us bread. Exhausted and frustrated, I pushed on to
Chołmogory in search of justice. Walking the streets I came across a
big building, with a sign outside which identified it as a *Sud* – a court.

"Ah, here we go," I thought. "I'll go to the court, that's where I'll find justice." So I entered the building, and wandered round until I found a door marked *procuror*. "Aha," I thought, "a barrister, that's just what I need." I knocked and listened, until I heard "Come in." Although I was a little frightened, I went in and stood by the door. Behind the desk sat a man with a very kind face, and he beckoned to me with his hand, meaning for me to approach him.

Through my tears I told him everything, that mum was in hospital, that our bread ration had been withheld from us, that we were dying of hunger, and that the president of the *sovkhoz* had spurned my pleas for clemency. He listened to me very carefully, then picked up the telephone receiver. In a booming voice of rage, he unleashed a string of expletives to the person at the other end, then put down the receiver and very politely told me to return home and visit the president. We would have bread. Thanks to the intervention of that kind barrister, we were given not only our bread, but all the rations that had been withheld from us. What a feast we had that day, and what joy!

What hunger can make of you

For the person who has not known hunger, it is very hard to understand that the most degrading and debasing thing that can happen to a human is starvation. People who are suffering hunger cannot think about anything other than food – how, where and what to find to eat. Hunger makes humans into walking shadows, unthinking skeletons, humiliated, degraded and worthless. Hunger kills everything that is good, beautiful and noble in human beings. A hungry person loses all hope for a better tomorrow. He can't believe that a better future will come, and he stops believing in his right to live. He no longer feel like a human being, and he feels guilty that he is alive.

In such cases people often take their lives. Hunger is the biggest murderer of individuality and personality, and changes a human being into an unfeeling animal who cannot tear their thoughts from food. Enforced hunger is an awful form of slavery and warps people's personalities permanently. A poem by one of my friends who was also in Siberia, Katarzina Łukasiewicz-Price, can tell you more about this.

Sępy
W zadymionej izbie tłok się wielki robi,
Skostaniałe ręce wyciągają powoli
Gorącej wody, łyk jeden zda się
Przywróci siły, nie da zginąc woli.

Wokół stoją jakieś ludzkie cienie,
Przenoszą oczy na te straszne twarze
Co nie potrafią już czuć, ani mysleć
W tym ponurym mroku, w tej cuchnącej parze.

Dreszcz mnie przechodzi, ból serce przebija,
Gdzież jest ten człowiek wielki i wspaniały,
Gdzie rozum jego, gdzie wola, intelekt,
Gdzie wzniosłe uczucia, wielkie ideały?

Zupa dymiaca wszystko zabrała
Oczy glodem zamglone, tylko jedno widzą,
Czapy futrzane stojących dozorców
I twarze czerwone co kopią i szydzą.

Stoją, stłoczone dziwne ludzkie strzępy,
Zbici, zduszeni, wymarli,
A wokół te twarze nienawistne i ponure, jak sępy
Co dusze z zywych wydarli.

Vultures

In a smoke-filled chamber a great crush is forming; skeletal hands stretch out slowly; just one sip of hot water might restore your strength, prevent your will from dying.

Human shadows circle them, staring in and fixing their eyes on these frightful faces who are unable either to feel or think in this gloomy darkness, in this stinking steam.

A chill shivers through me, the pain in my heart is bursting; where has this great and splendid person gone? Where is his mind, where his will, his intellect, what has become of his lofty thought, his great ideals?

The steaming soup took everything from you. Eyes glazed by hunger, they see only one thing, the fur hats of their guards, their faces red, kicking and mocking.

They stand, these crushed, strange, human remains, beaten, suffocated, lifeless; around them circle the hateful, gloomy faces, like vultures, who rip out the souls of the living.

Chapter 10 – The Union of Polish Patriots,
the Kościuszko Division, and Other Events of 1943-44

In April 1943, the Germans announced the discovery of the mass graves of 10,000 Polish officers murdered by the NKVD in Katyń. Diplomatic relations between Russia and Poland immediately broke down. Russia began to liquidate Polish diplomatic outposts in all territories of the Soviet Union, and arrested their employees, accusing them of spying and other activities against the Soviet Union. Our diplomatic outpost in Archangel was closed at this time; the help stopped, and the supply of parcels from abroad ceased.

Thank goodness that General Anders had already marched his army out of the Soviet Union. Now Wanda Wasilewska acted for the benefit of Polish people in exile. Various contrasting opinions exist on her actions, and many are negative because she was a Communist. Her husband was, at the time, deputy minister of foreign affairs in the Soviet Union, although by profession he was actually a dramatist. Wasilewska was also a writer, so they had a common interest in literature, and the Soviet authorities took their opinions into consideration. Whatever her shortcomings, as the founder of the Union of Polish Patriots (Zwionzek Patriotów Polskich, shortened to ZPP) in the Soviet Union, she enabled great patriotic and humanitarian endeavours. The ZPP was the only legal Polish advocacy group which was taken seriously by the Soviet government, and dispensed help and care to Polish people living in conditions beyond comprehension.

It was not only Poles who signed up to this Union. Other nationals who had been Polish citizens before the war now declared themselves as Polish nationals. In this way, the ZPP tried to drag as many Poles as possible back from the far north of Siberia, and resettle them into different regions of the European part of the Soviet Union. Thanks to their efforts, from May to September 1944, the resettlement of exiles began – our people began to pour out from the regions of Archangel, Irkursk and Novosibirsk, from Krasnoyarsk, Stavropol and other regions, as far as Ukraine, the southern parts of Russia, Kursk, Rostov, Saratov, Voroniezh and Kiev. Exiles were settled into sugar factories and *sovkhozy*.

ZPP produced a newspaper in Polish called *Wolna Polska* (Free Poland). This was a weekly political and cultural magazine published in Moscow. Although it was strangled by the censors, it was in Polish and about Polish affairs, and this still meant a great deal. Thanks to Wanda Wasilewska, a new Polish army was organised in June 1943, the First Division "Tadeusz Kościuszko".

Colonel Zigmund Berring sent call-up cards to men from all corners of the Taiga. If they could, they then made their way to Kotlas, where new conscripts were given dry food, loaded onto train wagons and sent to a training camp in Siedlce on the river Oka. Here they formed the Kościuszko division. Training lasted from 15 July until 1 September, after which they marched to the front. From 12 to 15 October, the Kościuszko division took part in the battle of Lenino. The battle was unsuccessful, and the losses were colossal, thanks to poor training and leadership. After this battle, the division was withdrawn from the front line and sent to the second line. Anders' army was much better placed, because it was the first organised, better equipped, better trained and better fed. Only very weak people enlisted in the Kościuszko army, desperate to escape the labour camps or mines that constituted their homes in the deepest Taiga.

116

A booklet recording dues my mother paid for ZPP membership.

They were dressed in rags and unbelievably starved, but as long as they could still move and think they applied to the army. This was their *ostatnia deska ratunku*, the last chance for survival. They preferred to fight and die than continue living in the "Soviet Paradise". The Kościuszko division played a part in liberating Warsaw and then marched to Berlin. My Wujek Ignac and cousins Bolek and Janek Król joined the division. They were not killed in the Lenino battle, but did not all survive to see the end of the war. Wujek Ignac was killed in the battle for Warsaw. He had wanted more than anything to survive and get his wife and children out of Russia, but his dreams were not fulfilled. First his little girl Alinka died, and then his wife with a little son, left forever under the Taiga snow.

However, two of his children, Ludek and Basia, did survive and were placed in an orphanage in Russia. After the end of the war, all the children here were transferred to a Polish orphanage in Elbląg near the Baltic Sea. No-one was looking for these two poor abandoned children, but my sister Zosia worked tirelessly with the Red Cross to track them down. She then managed to get in touch with our other uncle, Stanisław Stasiak, who hadn't been exiled to Siberia with us (although he had been sent there during the reign of the Czars when he fought for a free Poland). Wujek Stanisław had recently been elected as a member of parliament for the new Polish government and therefore was in a

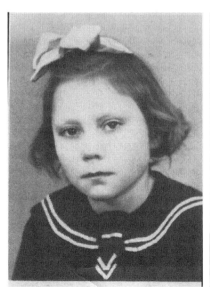

Basia and Ludek, shortly after leaving the Russian orphanage. Despite being still a child, Ludek was enlisted to the cadets.

position of influence. He removed his brother's children from the Elbląg orphanage. Ludek – who was just 11 years old – was enrolled into the military cadets; Basia, meanwhile, was placed in a boarding school in Warsaw.

Bolek Król managed to escape the hell of Soviet Russia and survive the war. He reached the rank of captain, and afterwards settled with his family in a village near Włocławek called Wistka Szlachecka, remaining with the new Polish army. They had another son, and christened him Ryszard, but as a nickname we called him Królewicz, or Prince – son of "King" Król. Life finally seemed all right… but, after making it through Soviet gulags for almost three years, after surviving fierce fighting in the front line against the Germans and after performing further military service for a free Poland, he could not bring himself to forgive Stalin, who sent thousands of Poles to their death, and whose policies caused Bolesław's own father Hipolit to die of hunger in Siberia.

At the christening party for Królewicz, Bolek complained loudly that his father had never returned from exile, and publicly accused Stalin of war crimes. One of his "friends" in attendence – who was, in fact, one of the godfathers of this child – denounced him to the Politburo. Almost immediately, Bolesław was arrested and thrown into the toughest prison in Kraków, where he was beaten and tortured by Communist Poles, often until he lost consciousness.

When he came out of prison and visited me in Bydgoszcz, he spoke to me in a whisper, checking all the walls to see if there were any listening holes. In this distracted and tragic fashion he told me about his experience. One of the techniques they had used on him was water

Bolek Król in 1945.

torture; he was forced to sit on a thin concrete block surrounded by cold water all night; he was deprived of sleep, because if he fell asleep he would fall into the freezing water. Moreover, while he was sitting on this block, drops of ice-cold water were dripped on his head, slowly but insistently and for long stretches of time.

After a while, he said, it felt like having rocks dropped on his head, not drops of water; each impact made him feel like his head was splitting open and he would faint. But of course each time he fainted, he would land in the bitterly cold pool. Revived in this brutal manner, wet and cold, he was forced to climb back up to his torture seat. He yelled in desperation but nobody came to rescue him. My cousin died very soon after his release.

Bolesław was rehabilitated by the Polish state, and was posthumously awarded a military cross; his wife was given a widow's pension. Thus ends the history of the hero of the Battles of River Oka and Lenino.

Fortunately, my Ciocia Hela's life turned out better. Her husband, Marcel Kitajewski joined Anders' army and, thanks to this, they escaped Soviet exile four years before us. Wujek Marcel, as a soldier of this army, had the right to take all his family with him, his wife and four children. Other soldiers in Anders' army were allowed to do the same. They took them to Iran first, where there was a military camp, with hospitals, a school and youth organisations. Young people could get themselves both a general education and a professional one. Anders not only rescued them from hell but he organised a new life for them.

Unfortunately not everything was good in the Anders camp, because the climate of the lands through which they travelled was terribly different and hard, in a totally different way from the north of Russia and Siberia. These people arrived in Iran completely exhausted by the long journey, and large numbers fell ill with typhus, a wave of illness connected with food poisoning, and began to die there as well. My Ciocia Hela told me about this herself; her little daughter Dzunia almost died of typhus. Thank God, everything turned out well for them in the end. They arrived in England in 1947 and settled in London, where their oldest daughter Urszula and their son Ryszard are still living. Wujek Marcel, a hero of Anders' army, died at an advanced age, and Ciocia Hela died in 2005 at the age of 100. Their son Ludomir settled in Belmont, California, and their daughter Camilla in Bel Air.

Two songs about the river Oka

Soldiers of the Kościuszko Division made up songs about the river Oka, comparing it to the Wisła (known as the Vistula in English), Poland's longest river, which crosses the country from the mountains in the south to the Baltic Sea in the north. They marched to Poland through battles and through blood, singing this song in the face of death:

1. Szumi dokoła las
Czy to jawa, czy sen?
Co ci przypomina, co ci przypomina,
Widok znajomy ten?

2. Był już nie jeden las
Wiele przeszlismy rzek.
Ale najpiękniejszy, ale najpiękniejszy,
Jest naszej Wisły brzeg.

3. Złoty wiślany piach,
Wioski słomiany dach,
Płynie, płynie Oka,
Jak Wisła szeroka, jak Wisła głęboka.

1. The forest hums around us; is this real or a dream? What does it remind you of – a familiar view, perhaps?

2. We've not only known one forest; we've crossed many a river. But the most beautiful of all, is our Wisła riverbank!

3. Ah, Wisła's golden sand, and thatched rooves in the villages. This Oka flows just like the wide, deep Wisła.

I found another poem about the Oka, "Ballada O żołnierzu tułaczu", in a book by Jan Prorok, *Skazani na zagłade*. I transcribe its powerful first two stanzas here, as I contemplate the displacement of my family.

> *Tam, gdzie Oka za zakrętem,*
> *Mruga w słoncu okiem Wisły*
> *Przysiadł tułacz nad odmętem*
> *I o Polsce się zamyslił.*
> *Jak do Ciebie skrócić droge?*
> *Jak odnalezć scieżki hoże?*
> *Spod Kołymy znad Pieczory*
> *Do Warszawy? – Poradź Boże!*
>
> *Ojciec w lesie z głodem walczy,*
> *Brat z Andersem już w Iranie,*
> *Czy mnie jeszcze sił wystarczy,*
> *Aby do Niej dotrzeć, Panie?*

There where the Oka rounds a bend,
Blinking in the sun with the eye of the Wisła
A wanderer sat contemplating its depths,
And thinking about Poland.
How can I shorten my way to you?
How to find the perfect path
From Kołyma, from the river Pieczora,
To Warsaw? Advise me, God!

My father is fighting hunger in the forest
My brother has gone with Anders to Iran,
Will I have enough strength
To return to her, O Lord?

Resettlement from the northern Soviet Union to Ukraine and European USSR

At the beginning of 1944, the ZPP applied for the resettlement of 26,885 Poles and Jews from the far north and Siberia to Ukraine.[3] From May to September 1944 the resettlement took place. Prisoners were released from jails and gulags, although no doubt not all of them. But they released my uncle and my brother, as I have already mentioned, when my Ciocia Andzia, Balbina and I went to get them from the Archangel gulag.

I don't remember when exactly they loaded us onto the train, but I remember that the wagons were cattle wagons – except not locked up this time, their large doors were open. The train pulled along slowly and frequently stopped in fields. Passengers climbed out for toilet breaks, because there were no holes in the floor in the wagons, as there had been before in the Russian *eszelon* from Poland. Everyone was happy about being able to leave the wagons freely, but you had to be careful, because the trains could start moving without warning! I remember how I barely managed to reach my wagon once as the train pulled off. Running as fast as we could, we literally had to leap in – people reached out to grab my outstretched hands. If they hadn't, I would have ended up in a field without money or documents. It would have been worse than the time something similar had happened to Zosia, because she was older than me, and at least she had bread and her documents.

The wagons were packed with people, and they were dirty and lice-ridden. I remember how people's hair looked white from the lice

[3] According to a statistic from Wanda Niezgoda-Górska, *Dosyć nam Sybiru, dosyć Kazachstanu* (1994).

eggs, and how the big lice were crawling around on people's clothes and bodies. But this time we were not hungry. They gave us some bread for the journey, and even some money so we could buy something at stops and stations. Russian women stood on the platforms with baskets of food and tea, and shouted, *Pirozhki! Chai!* – Dumplings and tea! It turned out that these good women were giving out dumplings for free. They were very tasty and smelled beautiful. It was a real treat.

We travelled for a long time until in the end we got to our destination. At the station, foremen waited for us with carriages, onto which we put our luggage. We sat there too, and they carried us, not to the forests this time, but to the collective and state farms, and sugar factories. They settled us in a *sovkhoz* called Radomlia. Our new address was:

> *Sumskaia oblast',*
> *Trostianiets'kii raion*
> *sovkhoz Radomlia.*

CHAPTER 11 – UKRAINE, *SOVKHOZ* RADOMLIA

The chairman of this *sovkhoz* was a Polish Jew, called Sigizmun Sigizmunowicz. He was a middle aged man of a solid build with Semitic features. He lived there with his wife and daughter Zosia. They spoke Polish well, both he and his wife. Sigizmun was very good to us Poles. Bringing us to the *sovkhoz* they located us in the upstairs rooms of the social club. Downstairs was a canteen and a big dining room, where *sovkhoz* workers came to eat. Upstairs was a hall with a stage, where before our arrival they hosted meetings, lectures, films and dances. When we arrived, we too this club hall over as living quarters. Our family were on the stage, and we were very happy with it. Under the stage we had a lot of room for our things and for firewood. There we even kept a beautiful white rabbit, which was given to my brother Tadzio by a Ukrainian lady.

In the downstairs room two families were settled, five people in one corner, three in another. There were also five of us on our stage, with thirteen people in the room as a whole. It was okay. There was only one stove to heat the whole apartment. Later on, they built a little stove, joined to the big stove, for us to cook on.

The Michalczuk family had two daughters, Genia and Lodzia and a son Kazik, the same age as my brother Tadek. They took one corner of the hall, and in the other corner was a widow of a forester. She was a White Russian called Mrs Protasiewicz. She had a little son called Bobik, and her step-daughter Wala (aged around 12 to 14), who Mrs Protasiewicz always beat and insulted. Fortunately Wala's uncle, her father's brother, eventually took her away.

In front of the social club were benches, where Ukrainian youth sat and enjoyed themselves. They played guitars, balalaikas and harmonicas. They sang harmonious Ukrainian songs and danced beautifully. We went out to them to meet them and learned to sing and dance to Ukrainian songs. They were all very nice and sincere to us. When they brought us to Ukraine it was still fully summer. It was very warm and smelled beautifully of ripening crops. On one side of our *sovkhoz* was a deep and wide valley, overgrown with flowing bushes and trees. There were many such woods in this area, with lots of fruit trees – apples, pears, plums, all very sweet and juicy – and you could go and pick them yourself because they belonged to nobody, only nature.

In our *sovkhoz*, soldiers from Kościuszko Division were stationed as they prepared themselves for the front. Sigizmun Sigizmunowicz arranged a beautiful farewell for them. I don't remember, but maybe this farewell coincided with 1 May, when we also had big celebrations, maybe he did it specially, but the party was absolutely out of this world. Tables were placed outside, and they were full of wonderful food – sausage, ham from American parcels, bread, tomatoes, cucumbers, fruit, cakes, whatever you could wish for. (Of course there was also a lot of vodka!)

For us, this was heaven on earth! For four years we had faced starvation, and now we didn't know what to take from the tables, it was like something from a fairy tale. There was also an area where people played and danced, and soldiers were singing, including one women soldier who sang solo. We were extremely contented and happy then –we had met real genuine people, and could hear Polish conversations, Polish songs and could see with what happiness our own dear Polish soldiers were preparing for departure to the front. They were going to fight the enemy and win the war so that Poland would be free and our families would be able to return back home, and life would be back to normal.

Here is what my sister wrote on the subject:

"Our soldiers took care of us before they departed. They brought us a delicious pea and ham soup and tasty bread, and butter and ham. The Captain asked me whether I would go with them as a secretary. He wanted me to join his unit, but I refused. I asked him that instead of me he would take my brother Zdzichu and that they would leave him at our uncle near Lublin, because they were going to go that way. My brother was still young, he was only 20. He was missing two fingers on his right hand, and because of this injury he couldn't be included in the army, but that was good because it meant he couldn't be killed in battle. My Wujuk Ignac was killed in the battle of Warsaw. When his army passed Lublin, he managed to visit his sister Fela. She later told me that he had visited them when the army was passing through Markuszów; they had tried to persuade him to stay with them, promising him that they would hide him until the end of the war, if necessary. But wujek didn't even want to listen to such proposals. He went with the army, and he died."

How many died in the battle of Warsaw? History can tell you that: much has been written in recent years about this awful event.

We were very grateful that Captain Domański took my brother to Lublin where our uncle Władek Stasiak had a big farm and a brick-making factory in nearby Dys. When my brother had rested, he found a job for himself in Lublin in Polish radio. So at least one was already saved in our family – and we joined him in March 1946, when they brought us back to Poland. The farewell to the Polish army was enormously touching – for some very happy, for some very sad. There were many bitter tears shed as well. The Ukrainian women were saying goodbye to their Polish lovers, but we were crying with happiness for our brother Zdzichu. The army departed, leaving broken hearts and other bitter consequences, which I will relate later.

The soldiers left and normal life began. Autumn approached, the crops were harvested and processed. We wandered around fields picking up the leftover ears of corn. My sister went to work. Mum was not able to, because she had still had her secondary invalid status. My brother Tadzio and I started to go to Ukrainian school. They assigned us to the fourth year of primary school – when I left Poland I had been in the fourth year, and now here I was again, four years later. What great educational progress I had in the Soviet Union!

The school was led in Ukrainian. The children were of different ages. Some of them were repeating the third year in the same class. The teacher, Elizawieta Pietrowna, praised us very highly, and presented us as an example to her Ukrainian students. It wasn't hard for us to learn. We had various subjects – maths, history, biology geography, Russian and Ukrainian language, singing and military training. A soldier came to our lessons and taught us about the construction of a rifle, and what it was for. To this day I remember his definition of a rifle: *vintovka boitsa do porazheniia vraga – ognem, shtykom, i prikladom* – a soldier's gun to kill the enemy – with gunfire, with the bayonet or with the butt.

It was great to go to school up till winter. In winter it was cold, and we didn't have boots or warm clothes. Fortunately our teacher was the daughter of a very kind Ukrainian lady with whom we became friendly soon after the Polish army left. So Elizawieta Pietrowna took me to her house for the winter. She lived in the school with her son, Wowa, and her husband was in the front lines. In free times between classes I looked after her son. I told him stories, and sang him songs, and he taught me this poem: *Kto-to k slivkam podobralsia, kotik, ty ne vinovat? Ty naverno, brat, priznaesh'sia, a nie priznashsia, plokho, brat!* – "Someone's been at the cream / Surely it's your fault little cat? / I'm sure it's you / Own up to it my dear / Because if you don't, it'll be all the worse for you!"

Elizabieta Pietrowna was always cooking something nice, but the thing I liked most was *tushenaia tsebula* – slices of onion between slices of potatoes, with milk or cream that was then half-fried, half-steamed in the oven. It was very tasty; up to this day the thought of it makes me salivate. Once, she asked me to cook something Polish. What to do? She had lots of potatoes, so I made her potato dumplings, *pyzy*. She liked them a lot, and she called them *galushki*. I enjoyed life at my teacher's house; I learned a lot thanks to her. By the end of the year 1945 I was awarded a certificate, which was later accepted in Poland when I was applying to teacher training college in Bydgoszcz.

Pictures taken when I was at teacher training college in Bydgoszcz.

Our Chairman, Sigizmun Sigizmunowicz, helped us a great deal, and gave us various food products whenever we asked him for them, or at least gave us the certificates we needed to get them from the shop. When it was Christmas Eve, Tadek and I went to him to sing Polish carols. He invited us into his house, and listened to our singing with tears in his eyes. Afterwards he offered us *pierogi* with meat and gave us some wine. I will never forget this good man. Obviously, he was too good to people, because the Commissariat found a deficit in his stock, and it looked like he was going to be gaoled. He knew that if he went to prison he would never come out, so he took his own life.

By the time of his death, it was winter. Poles from our *sovkhoz* made him a giant wreath from pine tree branches. Everyone was very upset that he died. Fortunately, our departure to Poland gave us the opportunity to take his wife and daughter Zosia with us. There were many good people in Ukraine. Soon after our arrival in that country, my sister and I went to our district town, Trostianiec, to see the dentist. In the waiting room, we spoke to a very nice Ukrainian lady, called Mrs Fyedorkina. She said to us: *"Devushki, vy ne zdzeshnie, otkuda vy?"* – "Girls, you are not local, where are you from?" We said that we were displaced Polish "immigrants", that we'd come from the Archangel region, and that we now lived in Radomlia. She told us that she lived in the village Pticznaja, just next to our *sovkhoz*. She had three sons, a cow, chickens and a patch of land adjoining her house. The rest of her land was taken from them and given to the *sovkhoz*. One son, Vasiliy, was a lieutenant in the army and was serving on the front. A second son, Vanya, was 18 and still studying, while the third, Szura, went to the same school as Tadzio and I.

She invited us to her house, and from that time gave us two litres of milk every day for free. *Co to był za raritas!* – What a great luxury! It was unbelievably delicious. After four years, at last we could smell that we were drinking real milk, and have a cup for supper with a chunk of rye bread. This was, for us, the best of all possible medicines. Mrs Fyedorkina introduced us to another lady who also lived in our area, Mrs Kozachenko, the mother of my teacher, who was unbelievably good to us.

In return for their many kindnesses, Tadzio offered to look after their cows during his holidays. Other people heard about this, and asked him to look after theirs cows, too. For this, they gave him various products, and even a bit of money. So our summer in Ukraine was good for us. I began to visit Mrs Kozachenko, either by myself or with my mother, to help in their gardens, or with some needlework. Mrs Kozachenko had sent two sons to the front lines. The younger, Pasza, had been a musician, and played on the bandura, an old Ukrainian instrument. She showed us this instrument, and was very proud of him; he had been killed in action, and she would weep whenever she told us about him. Her other son, Wasja, was a captain in the army, and returned after the end of the war. He spoke very badly about the Poles, saying that he and his fellow Ukrainians had given their lives to free Poland from the German occupation, but the Poles hated them, and threw bricks at them, calling them Russians.

Wasja had a wife, who was a dentist, and they had a son. His wife fell in love with a Polish officer, who promised her that he would take her to Poland with him, or return for her if he had to leave without her. I don't know if he did, but I suspect not. Her husband returned from the army and found out about her romance, so he beat her up terribly; people said that he even smashed his guitar over her. Then he left her and his son; he got together with another girl, who he brought with him from the front! So you see how it is – men are allowed to get away with anything, but a woman can't!

From Mrs Kozachenko, I learnt many beautiful Ukrainian songs. She was always singing, and when she sang certain songs she would cry. Ukrainians are a very musical people. They all sing and dance beautifully, and it seems that each person can play an instrument – whether scripki, harmoshka, guitara, balalaika or bandura. They sing on the way to work, on the fields before work, and on their way home. In the evening they would gather together outside the local club (where we lived) sitting on benches and would sing in various voices that interacted wonderfully with each other – sentimental songs or war songs, or *czastuszki*, short comical songs that they also danced to. We Poles also learnt to sing *czastuszki* and dance the *kozachok*.

Life was good and merry here. I had a Polish friend Nina Kulikowa, with whom I walked to school. Her mother was a fortune-teller who would read cards and palms. She told the fortunes of all the women whose husbands and lovers were on the front. They paid this fortune-teller a lot. I watched how this woman told her fortunes, and learnt to do it – I started to do it too. I made up a lot of it, but they always told me "You're right!" and would come back to me "Tell me more, tell me more, you're speaking the truth." Well, what could I do? I told them more, for which they would bring me *pierogi* filled with mushrooms, meat or fruit. Not bad for the wisdom of a seventeen-year-old.

On top of being a fortune teller, I also tried my hand at being a hairdresser. I came up with a variety of different hairstyles, and for this they also paid me with food. In the summer holidays, I worked in the kitchens. The manageress of the kitchen asked me to take over from her for two weeks because she wanted to go on holiday to Kurort, a spa in the Caucasus. I knew how to cook a few things, such as *kasza*, Ukrainian borsch and *shchi* (cabbage soup). They didn't ever cook anything else. She asked me to find a friend to help me, and I asked for Nina Kulikowa. We liked this work very much, and we felt proud and a little superior. We cooked these meals in enormous cauldrons, and gave out the dishes to the workers through a window. Everyone praised our cooking and us. We felt important and wanted to live.

My sister worked on the fields in summer, planting potatoes, weeding, harvesting, threshing corn or digging up potatoes and sugar beet. They put the potatoes into big trenches in the ground. The beet they dispatched to a sugar factory, while the vegetables that would go to the cows also went into the ground – first they would put in straw and soil to protect from frost.

There were many jobs in the *sovkhozy*, just like in any farm. My sister also acted as a sort of social worker for the Poles there. In Sumy (the city) a Polish Patriots Union was created, and this organised help for the exiled Poles, or Polish citizens who hadn't actually been born there. My sister was selected as a secretary of the local organisation. She writes:

"I was chosen secretary of the ZPP for our district. I would go once a month to their meetings, where I was given a programme of work. To organise Polish youth, provide lessons in writing and reading in Polish, to provide them with books and press materials (leaflets, articles etc). To organise cultural events, lessons in dancing and singing or physical education. I gathered the Polish youth and in this way I organised a little Polish school. Mr Stanisław Kols was chosen as the chairman of our organisation, and I was the secretary. Mr Kols was a great man and a clever Pole, and it was lovely to work with him. However, Mr Kulik was trying to disrupt things. He was a white Russian, and he didn't speak perfect Polish, but he had high ambitions, and thought he should teach the children Polish, not me.

As a result he gave me a lot of hassle, and he wouldn't deliver to me the correspondence from the main office in Sumy. Eventually, everything came out when I went to Sumy for a meeting. At that time Mr Kulik was still the chairman of our organisation, and Mr Kols was his deputy. At the main meeting when everything came out about what sort of man Kulik was, then the main chairman of the ZPP, asked my opinion about Kulik's replacement, and partly because I asked for Mr Kols he was chosen.

"Apart from organising the teaching of Polish children, I was going to Sumy for food and clothes that were sent from America and England as help for Poles. This was very dangerous work, because many bandits roamed the area who would fall on travellers and take their goods. This once happened to me.

"I received the gifts, and walked to the train with two suitcases. Two men approached me, one hit me in my hand with something heavy and when my suitcase fell he grabbed it. The other man grabbed the other suitcase and both were stolen. When I tried to beg them to leave me at least one, they flicked a knife in front of my eyes and I said no more, because I wanted to save my life. So I came home without the suitcases – but still alive.

"The next time I went with my friend to get these supplies. We were advised to go to the station slightly further away from the track along a ravine. So we did that and hid ourselves behind bushes. As the train was approaching, only then did we emerge. But now we were not by ourselves – there were two men, and together we were more brave, our return was much more successful, and everyone was happy with the things we brought back. At the end of 1945 we began to prepare to return to Poland, and I took my part in this, making lists of Poles according to families. I had to write a lot in Polish and in Russian, which wasn't difficult for me. I had attended agriculture college in Dubica, and I had taken a physical education course in Brześć. I knew Polish and Russian well.

"Some Poles left early, immediately after the end of the war. For example Mr Janek Logwinowicz was in Kościuszko's army, and after 9 May 1945 he came straight from Poland to get his wife, his mother and son. But there was nobody who could come and get us, and we had to stay one more winter there, and only in March 1946 could we finally stand again on Polish territory."

Waiting for departure

We waited patiently for our turn to leave. War was over, and Polish soldiers were coming to get their families. We were saying our farewells to those who were departing. Everything began to fill our hearts with hope and happiness. The worst thing was that many Russian and Ukrainian soldiers were in similar positions to us – i.e. coming home – and not all of them had good memories from Poland, just as Mrs Kozachenko's son had felt. The returning soldiers found out that young Polish girls lived in their *sovkhoz*, and they wanted to harm us. In other words they wanted to take revenge for their ill-treatment in Poland. In the evenings we would hear them gathering in front of our club saying they would show us what a Russian soldier could do. "We have freed you, and now we want to have some fun with Polish girls." We were very scared, and would no longer leave home in the evenings. But they would still gather outside their club, and through open windows we could hear everything they were saying.

I was the youngest, at 17, so my sister told me to hide myself under the stage, somewhere deep. My sister, a girl called Genia, and Lodzia, Mrs Protasiewicz and our "men" Tadzio and Kazio (both aged 14), started to barricade the door for the night. First they used slide-locks, then hooks, then they pulled across various tables, benches and anything else we had, to make it impossible for them to get in if they tried to break the door down. The girls had axes ready too. Late one night, they knocked on the door. On our side, no-one said anything. They started to bang again, bashing and pushing on the door for a long time, accompanying their drunken attack with the worst sort of Russian swearing. Fortunately the doors were very sturdy, with strong locks, so they didn't even shake. Suddenly everything went quiet. For a while you could hear some noises and laughter and running down the stairs.

We thought that now they would start trying to get in through the windows. But they would have needed ladders to do this. Obviously they had decided to give up their attempts, and left. Nevertheless, not one of us had a moment's sleep that night, except Mrs Protasiewicz's boy, Wowik, who slept through the whole thing.

Only in the morning did the girls open the door and see "the high culture of the Soldier of the Red Army". They couldn't rape us, so they made a toilet under our door, and in this manner showed us what they were made of. We had to tell the police about this, and they said they would ensure that we would never see a repeat of this. They were right, nothing ever did happen again, but from that moment on we were very scared of former soldiers who had returned from the front.

From September, Tadzio and I started to go to fifth form, in a different school, a secondary school, which was situated in the regional town Trostianiec, quite far from our *sovkhoz*. Youngsters in this school were of various ages, from 12 to 20, or more. In my class there were both older and younger children. Your age didn't make any difference, nobody laughed at anybody else. The teachers always praised us Poles. In this school we started learning German. I liked it here, but unfortunately we only had three months there because the winter arrived. There were vicious frosts, and of course no transport – we had to walk to schol. For a while we used skis, but even that had to stop, because we didn't have enough warm clothes. So we stayed at home and awaited our transport to Poland.

138

An international agreement in the matter of repatriation of Poles was signed on 6 July 1945, but we only saw the results of it later on, at the beginning of 1946. Repatriation took place in turns, so not everyone went at once. The main first wave came in February 1946, and we were transported to Poland. The journey lasted a whole month, but it was a happy time. We were in open cattle wagons and we could leave – you just had to make sure the train didn't leave without you.

We arrived in Poland 14 March 1946. We had finally made it home.

This picture was taken in 1948, after our family settled in Sitno, Poland. In the back row are Zosia, Józia (carrying Zosia's son Rysiu), Zosia's husband Franek and his mother. In the front, one of Franek's cousins, me, Balbina and Zdzichu.

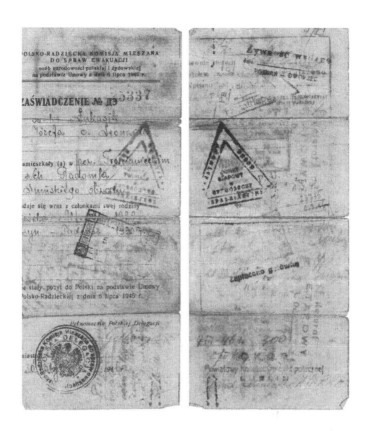

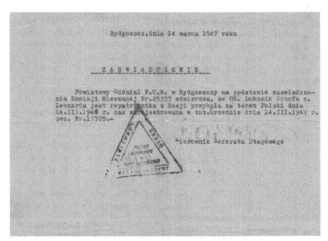

Top left and right, my Russian passport.
Bottom, confirmation of our arrival back into
Poland 14 March 1946 (registered 1947).

140

Some pictures of me as a young woman after surviving six years in the "Soviet Paradise". I qualified as a teacher in 1950 and worked in Poland until I came to England in 1963.

In 1969 my Diploma from the University of Kraków was recognised
in the UK, qualifying me to teach Russian in sixth form colleges.
I retired at 65, when I decided to write this book.

142

ABOUT THE AUTHOR

Alfreda Starża-Miniszewska moved to England in 1963, where she was a teacher of Russian for many years. A mother, grandmother and great-grandmother, she is now retired and lives in Derbyshire.

ACKNOWLEDGEMENTS

The author and translator would like to express their thanks to Matthew Kelly for commenting on an early draft, Terry Tagnazian for her advice about publication, Mel Bach for assistance with transliteration and Jaroslav Nejedlý for his considerable help designing the cover.

FURTHER READING

The author's cousin Ludomir Kitajewski recorded his memories of Siberia in *Journey into the Unknown* (2001), and the two books now stand as companions to one another.